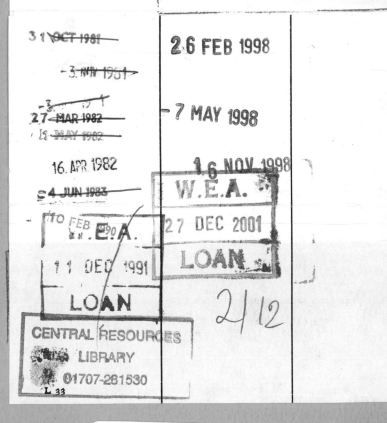

X-RAYING
THE PHARAOHS

X-RAYING THE PHARAOHS

*James E. Harris
and Kent R. Weeks*

Illustrated with Photographs

MACDONALD · LONDON

To the members of
the Egyptian Department of Antiquities,
past and present,
whose interest and assistance made possible
the x-raying of the pharaohs

CONTENTS

CONTENTS

PREFACE

X-Raying the Pharaohs is an account of the work done so far by an expedition under the direction of the University of Michigan's School of Dentistry. It is written for those people who have a general interest in the development of a field that, not many years ago, did not even exist. Technical terminology has been kept to a bare minimum in this book, and we hope that specialists in the various fields discussed will forgive us for sometimes cursorily treating problems we know to be important and highly controversial. They will find detailed treatment of these problems in the forthcoming *Roentgenographic Atlas of the Pharaohs*.

There is no problem more frustrating to writers on Egyptology or their readers than the lack of standardization in the spelling of personal names. Thutmosis, for example, may also be written as Tuthmosis, Thoutmose, or even Djehuty-mes; Amenhotep may appear as Amunhotep or Amunhotpe. The spellings used in *X-Raying the*

Pharaohs have been chosen because they are those most likely to be recognized by non-specialists, those most commonly used in the literature, or those most easily pronounced by speakers of English. The spelling of Arabic names is also somewhat arbitrary, and the Abd el-Rassoul mentioned in the text is the same as the Abd er-Rasol found in several of the quotations. The reader who may wish to learn more about Egypt's ancient rulers is advised to use his imagination when consulting the indexes of other texts.

A book treating so many subjects of such specialized nature is necessarily the result of many hands and many conferences. The dentists on the expedition, Dr. Harris, Dr. Ponitz, and Dr. Storey, have provided analyses of dental pathology; the radiologist, Dr. Whitehouse, data on the post-cranial skeleton; Mr. Russell, the x-rays upon which all work was based. To them and their staff goes the credit for the medical discoveries reported in this book.

Dr. Zaki Iskander, formerly director of Scientific Services and now director-general of the Egyptian Antiquities Department, has prepared a major study of mummification for the *Atlas,* and Chapter II of this book is an abridged version, with minor additions, of that article.

Dr. Harris, the director of the expedition, had charge of the entire project and made the final selection of data and interpretations to be included. Dr. Weeks is responsible for the Egyptological data, the translations of papyri, and, to insure continuity in the text, for the writing of the final draft of the book.

All of us on the expedition would like to pay special thanks to colleagues who have given so freely of their time to answer and discuss our many questions. We should particularly like to thank Dr. W. M. Krogman and Dr. Edward F. Wente for their invaluable contributions, and the administrative staff of the Egyptian Antiquities Department and the University of Alexandria School of Dentistry for allowing the project to be undertaken.

We believe there is a strong argument to be made for putting a non-technical report such as this in the hands of a general audience as soon as possible after a project is completed. We hope this book will justify that belief.

Members
of the Expeditions

THE MICHIGAN EXPEDITION

James E. Harris, D. D. S., University of Michigan
Kent R. Weeks, Ph. D., American University in Cairo
Paul V. Ponitz, D. D. S., University of Michigan
Arthur Storey, Ph. D., D. D. S., University of Toronto
Walter Whitehouse, M. D., University of Michigan
William Russell, Radiological Technician,
    University of Michigan

UNIVERSITY OF ALEXANDRIA COLLABORATORS

Abdel Rahman el-Sadr, M. D., Vice-Rector
Mohammed Abdalleh, D. D. S., Dean, School of Dentistry
Khadry Galil, D. D. S., Demonstrator
Samir Abu el-Zam, D. D. S., Demonstrator
M. Samir Loutfy, D. D. S., former Demonstrator

EGYPTIAN MUSEUM AND ANTIQUITIES DEPARTMENT STAFF

Gamal Moukhtar, Ph. D., Undersecretary of State

Gamal Mehris, Ph. D. (deceased), Director-General,
    Antiquities Department

Henry Riad, Ph. D., Director, Egyptian Museum

Zaki Iskander, Ph. D., Director, Technical Services (now
    Director-General), Antiquities Department

Mohammed Abd el-Mohsen, Curator, Egyptian Museum

Ibrahim el-Nawawy, Assistant Curator, Egyptian Museum

Saniyya Abdelal, Assistant Curator, Egyptian Museum

A PORTFOLIO
OF PICTURES

The pictures on the following four pages were selected to illustrate the variations in color which resulted from different techniques of mummification. Color is often a clue to the technique used and therefore to the period.

ABOVE: *Nefer*
LEFT: *Thutmosis I*
BELOW: *The Lady Imenit*

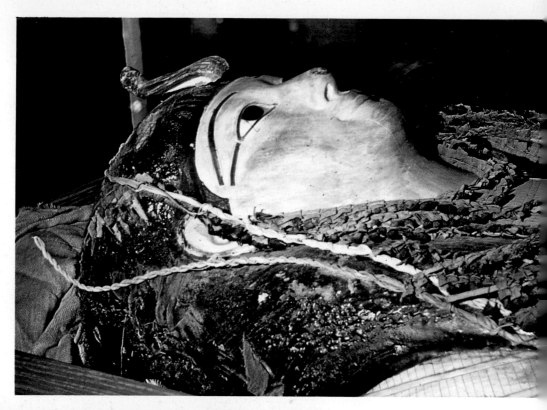

ABOVE: *Amenhotep I*
LEFT: *Seti I*

OPPOSITE, TOP: *Yuya*
OPPOSITE, BOTTOM
LEFT: *Yuya (abdomen, showing gold plate over embalmers' incision)*
OPPOSITE, BOTTOM
RIGHT: *Thuya, wife to Yuya*

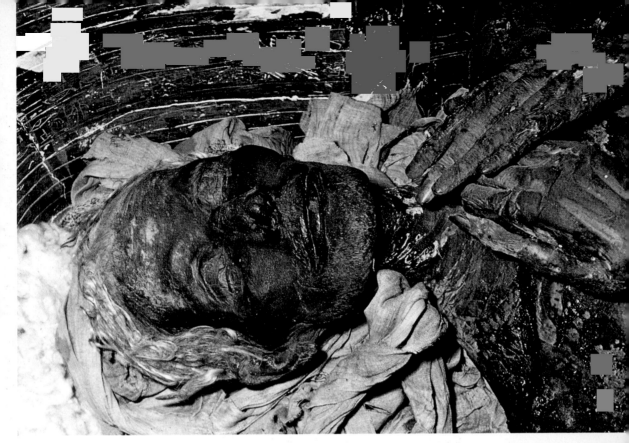

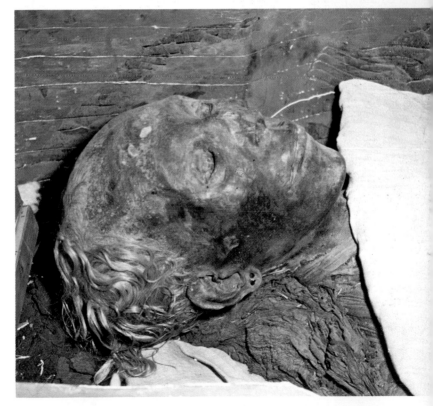

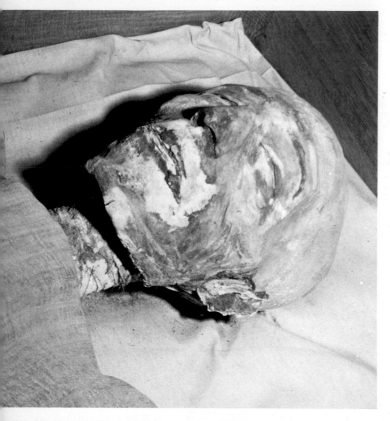

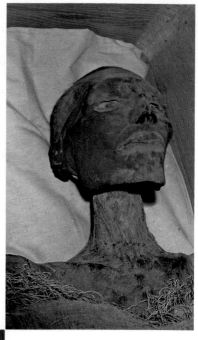

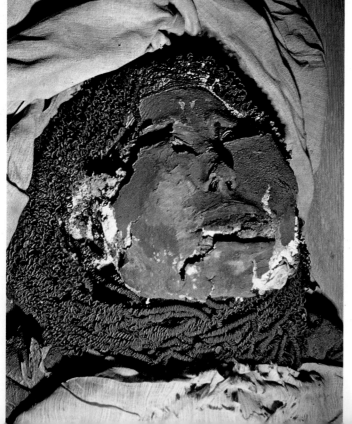

ABOVE, LEFT: *Merenptah*
ABOVE, RIGHT: *Ramesses V*
LEFT: *Queen Henttowy*

The Egyptian Museum in Cairo preserves one of the largest collections of mummies in the world, and the only collection of royal mummies. The collection, often thought to be merely a curiosity, is actually an important source of historical information. Mummies constitute only one part of an extensive funerary procedure which reflects both the deep religious convictions of the Egyptian people and their fondness for life in the valley of the Nile. These people believed in life after death and in the existence of spirits which had to be accommodated in the body. Hence the body had to be preserved for eternity as a home for these spirits, and provision for the foods and activities that made life pleasant in this world had to be placed in the tomb or represented in paintings and sculpture. To archaeologists, the tomb has become a museum preserving the history and the culture of ancient Egypt.

The mummies themselves are biologic museums, from which much can be learned about the physical appearance of the early Egyptians, their diseases, their life span, their knowledge and use of medicine, and the techniques they used in mummification. Careful study of the mummified kings even reveals something of the philosophy of the artists and sculptors who portrayed them in the temples and in their tombs.

The mummy collection in the Egyptian Museum was first studied from the anatomic viewpoint by Gaston Maspero and Elliot Smith in the 1880s and early 1900s. Now the radiographic survey of the ancient pharaohs, priests, nobles, and queens provides for the first time a view of mummies never unwrapped. The face is revealed; magic amulets of gold and semiprecious stones appear beneath the resin-covered wrappings; disease, old healed fractures, and even the age at death are still evident in the bones. The pictures that follow indicate the breadth of the information that may be gained from a study of the x-rays of the pharaohs and their court.

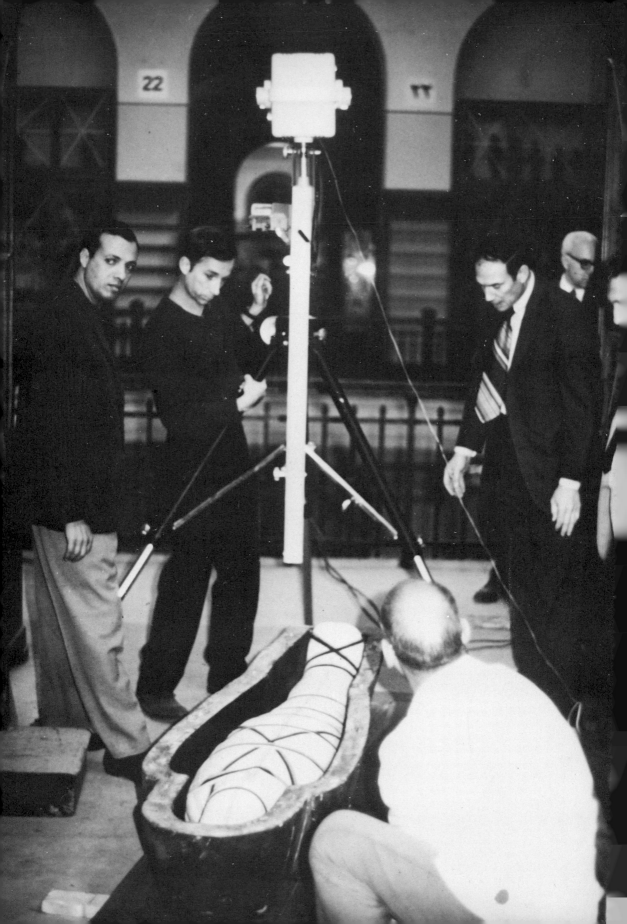

The Michigan-Alexandria research team x-rays an unwrapped mummy of the Late Dynastic Period on a second-floor gallery of the Egyptian Museum, which contains the only collection of mummies of the great pharaohs of the New Kingdom and their wives. The suggestion that this invaluable collection should be investigated through the use of x-rays was first made by Elliot Smith in 1912. The portable x-ray equipment has been positioned here to take conventional full-body medical x-rays, similar to those made in a modern hospital.

The mummy of Nefer (SEE COLORPLATE) almost 5000 years old, still lies in the wooden sarcophagus in his tomb beneath the causeway of an ancient pyramid at Saqqara. This mummy of a nobleman is especially important because it is the finest example of the technique of mummification in the Old Kingdom. The lateral x-ray of the head of Nefer reveals large jaws and excellent teeth. Other x-ray studies at the Giza Necropolis have revealed that there was considerable homogeneity among the nobles of the Old Kingdom, in contrast to the tremendous variation observed in the New Kingdom pharaohs and their queens.

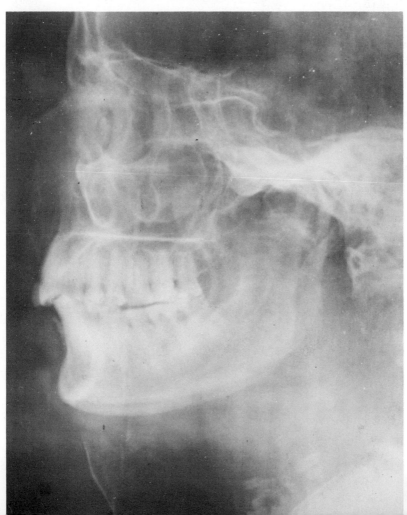

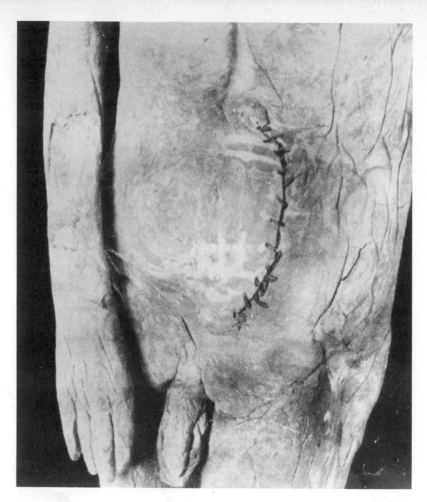

One of the procedures used in mummification was to remove the internal organs (except the heart). This was done through an incision made in the left groin, and the viscera were placed in four large canopic jars with lids carved to represent the Four Sons of Horus. This unwrapped mummy illustrates the technique; the large incision was sutured with string by the embalmers (after G. Elliot Smith and Warren R. Dawson, *Egyptian Mummies*, New York: Dial, 1923, plate XXXVI).

A radioactive isotope x-ray source was used to examine the extremely fragile mummy of the lady Imenit of the Eleventh Dynasty, Middle Kingdom (SEE COLORPLATE). In this mummy, unlike that of Nefer, the priests were not able to preserve a lifelike form. Mummification varied greatly through the history of ancient Egypt, and the technique is frequently an indication of the period in which the mummy was prepared. The x-ray plates dramatically reveal not only the facial skeleton but an extensive display of jewelry, much of it lying in disarray because of rough handling by tomb robbers.

24

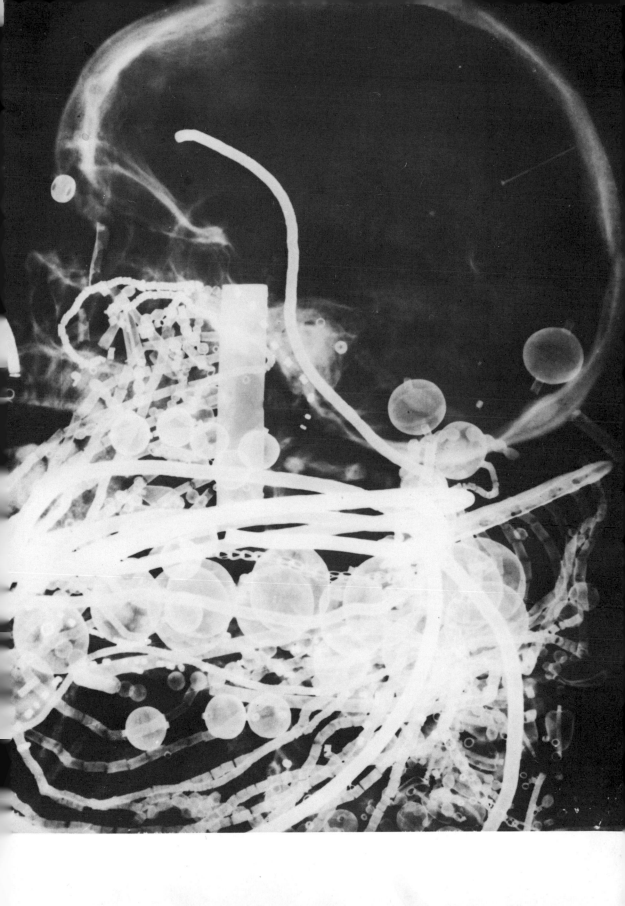

The long process of mummification, frequently taking seventy days, was followed by an elaborate funerary ceremony. The ceremony of burial shown here was probably sketched by a workman of the New Kingdom. While women stand at the top of the tomb shaft tearing their hair in mourning, a priest sprinkles incense, the body is lowered into a burial chamber containing two other mummies, presumably of the same family (from *Proceedings of the Society of Biblical Archaeology*, 1913, plate XLVI).

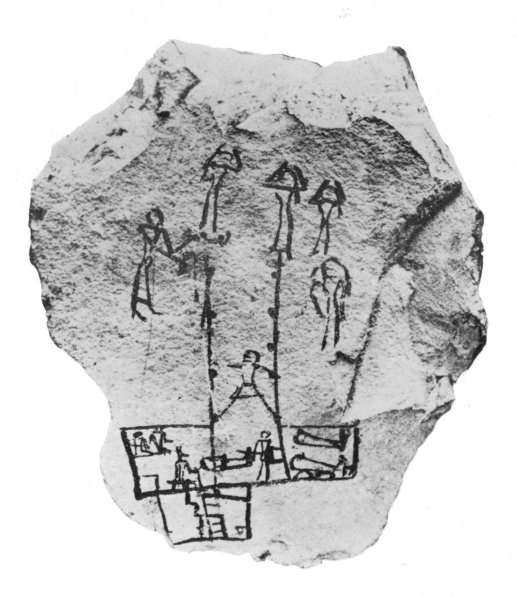

A belief commonly held in ancient Egypt was that a spirit called the ba *left the body after death in the form of a human-headed bird but at night returned to the mummy. Another spirit, the* ka, *remained with the mummy. The elaborate mummification procedures and the abundant funerary equipment found in the tombs were essential for the well-being of these spirits. A painting from the Late Dynastic Period shows the winged* ba *hovering over the mummy of Harsiesi, First Prophet of Horus at Edfou (courtesy of the Egyptian Museum, Cairo).*

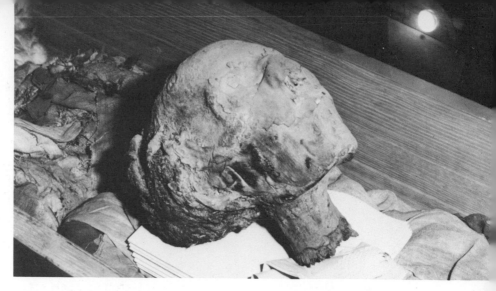

Not time but the extensive grave robberies in all periods of ancient Egypt caused the greatest damage to the mummified remains of the kings and queens. Many mummies were lost or their identification obscured after the violation of their tombs. This severed head of a mummy believed to be that of Tetisheri, wife of Senakhtenre Tao, a king of the Seventeenth Dynasty, is an example. The head has been positioned artificially to insure proper orientation to the x-ray machine, in order that the x-rays may be compared with known royal mummies of the same period. The lateral x-ray of the head reveals the marked maxillary protrusion (buck teeth) and the shape of the skull, remarkably similar to those in other women of this period. Remains of the brain at the back of the skull and an impacted third molar in the lower jaw may be identified.

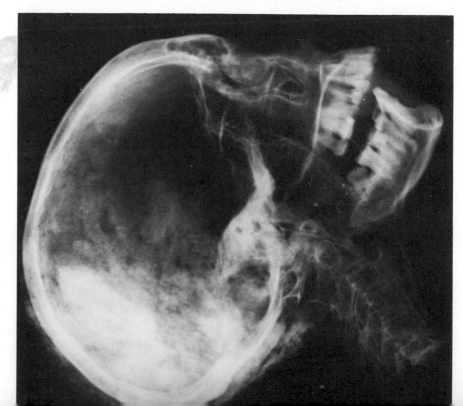

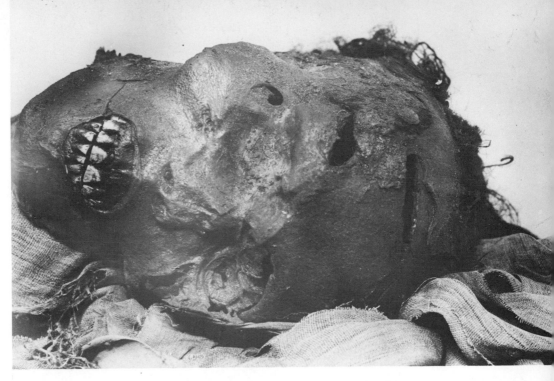

The resurgence of Egypt at the beginning of the New Kingdom has been associated with the driving out of the Hyksos from the Delta. Seqenenre Tao, a Seventeenth Dynasty ruler, is believed to have died in battle, and his mummy would seem to confirm this belief, since a horizontal ax wound and a large hole made by a blunt instrument in the forehead are readily visible. This is the only one of the collection of royal mummies that was not well preserved, a fact that was immediately noticeable when the glass case was removed. The lateral x-ray of the head reveals the details of the ax wound and the completely shattered cheekbone. If the ruler had survived any length of time, the x-rays would have revealed new bone formation and healing.

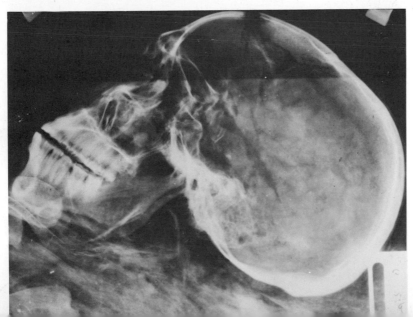

The pelvic x-ray of Ahmose I, son of Senakhtenre Tao, permits close inspection of morphologic detail frequently obscured by the heavy coating of resin. Of special interest is the discovery that, unlike most Egyptian males, Ahmose was not circumcised. It is tempting to suggest that this pharaoh was in ill health—perhaps even a hemophiliac or "bleeder."

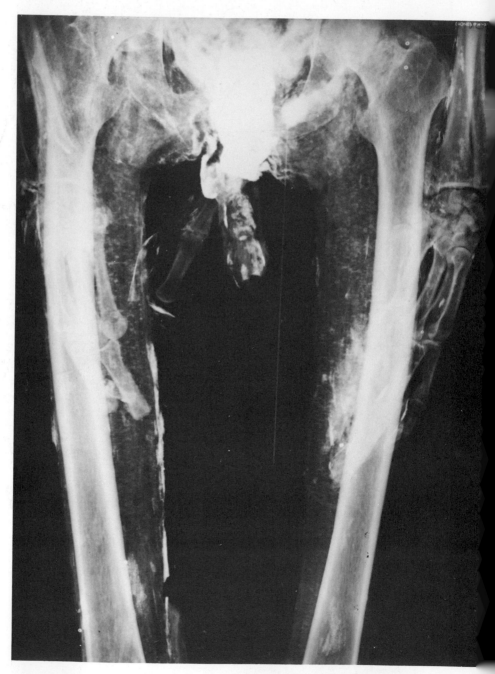

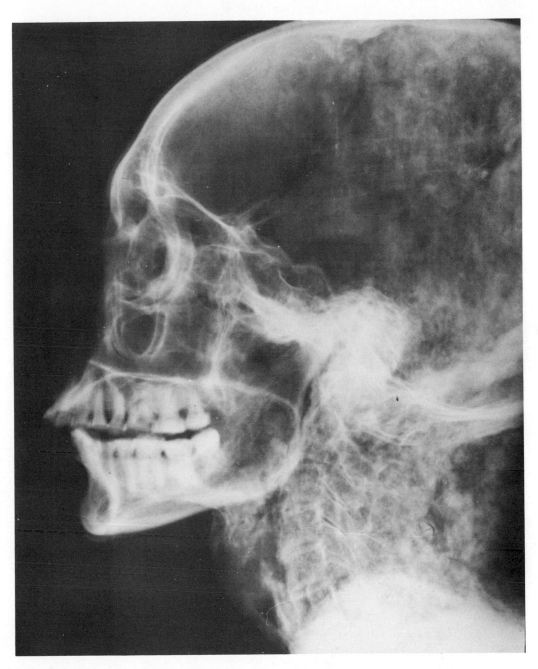

The lateral x-ray of Ahmose I's queen, Ahmose-Nefertiry, reveals the prominent protrusion already observed in Tetisheri and other early New Kingdom rulers and their families. The facial skeleton and the teeth provide a method by which family relationships can be evaluated.

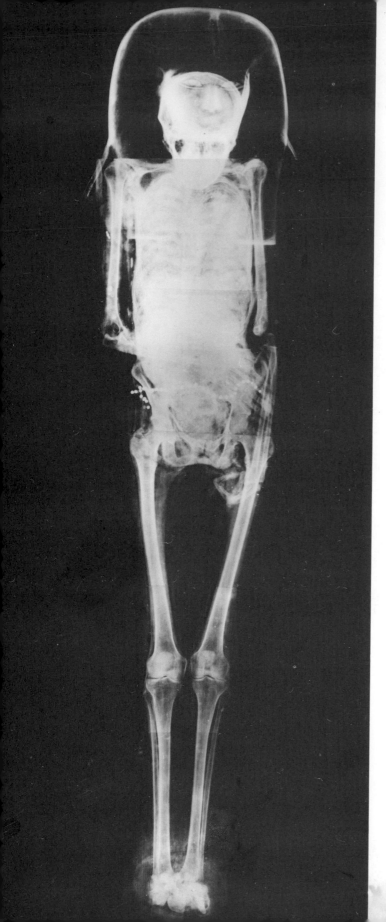

The beautifully wrapped mummy of Amenhotep I (SEE COLORPLATE) was in such an excellent state of preservation that earlier scholars did not unwrap it. The first glimpse inside the wrappings was provided by the x-rays taken in 1967. The mummy was revealed in its entirety by a series of overlapping x-ray film plates about 7.5 feet long (LEFT); the actual body is less than 5 feet 10 inches in height. The x-ray of the pelvic region (TOP, OPPOSITE) is especially important to Egyptologists. More significant than the belt of beads is the position of the arms. The lower left arm, separated at the elbow, is placed with the closed hand in the genital area; the lower right arm, with the hand showing a post-mortem fracture possibly caused by rewrapping by Twentieth Dynasty priests, is placed across the abdomen. The x-rays strongly suggest that the arms of this mummy, which had been greatly disturbed by tomb robbers, were originally crossed on the chest in the position frequent among royal mummies after Thutmosis I. The lateral head x-ray (OPPOSITE, BELOW) shows the features of the lifelike mask and the wrapped and mummified head beneath.

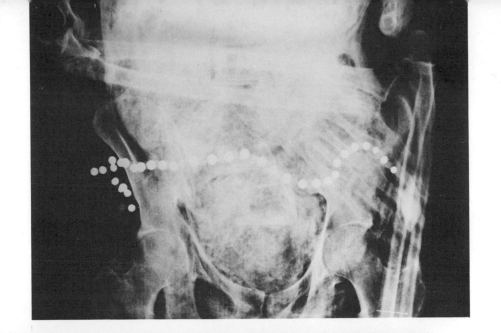

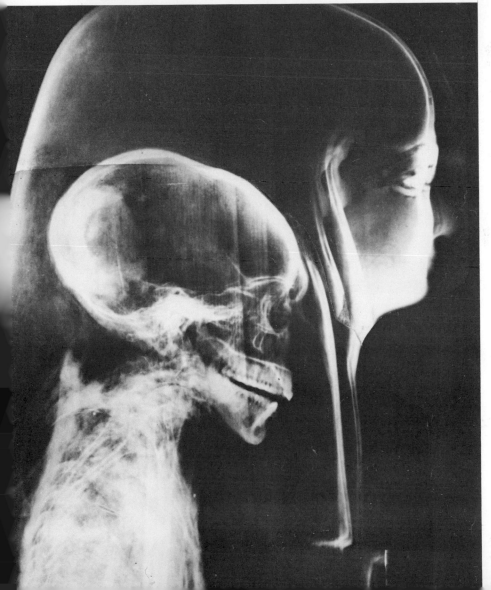

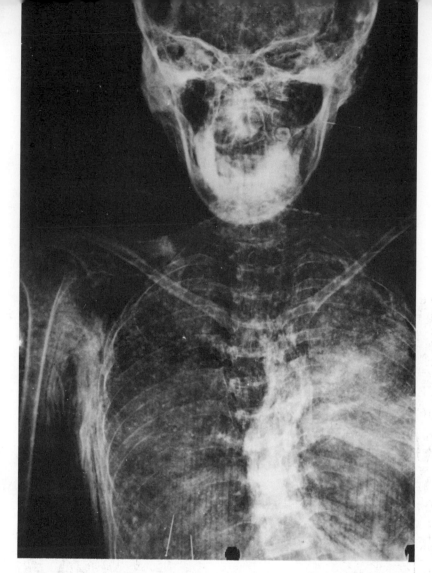

The x-ray investigation of the royal mummies is especially useful in the study of disease. The chest x-ray of Meryet-Amon, the wife and sister of Amenhotep I, reveals arthritis and scoliosis (abnormal curvature of the spine)—ailments also known to modern man.

The mummy (OPPOSITE, TOP) believed to be that of Thutmosis I is one of the best preserved of all royal mummies (SEE ALSO COLORPLATE). However, the identification has been questioned. The composite x-ray (OPPOSITE, BELOW) of the mummy identified as Thutmosis I reveals the hands clasped over the genitalia, in contrast to the pharaohs who succeeded him. The ends of the long bones in the legs had not closed, suggesting that this individual died before the age of eighteen, a fact which does not agree with the historical account of the length of Thut-mosis I's reign.

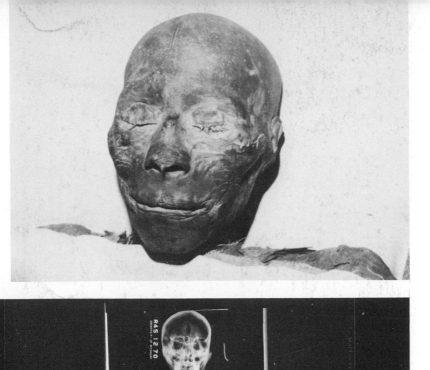

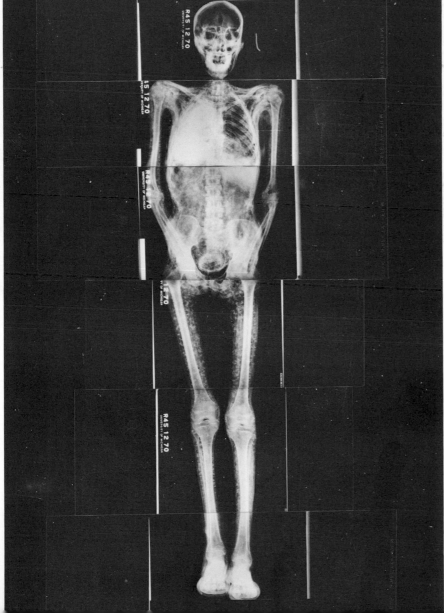

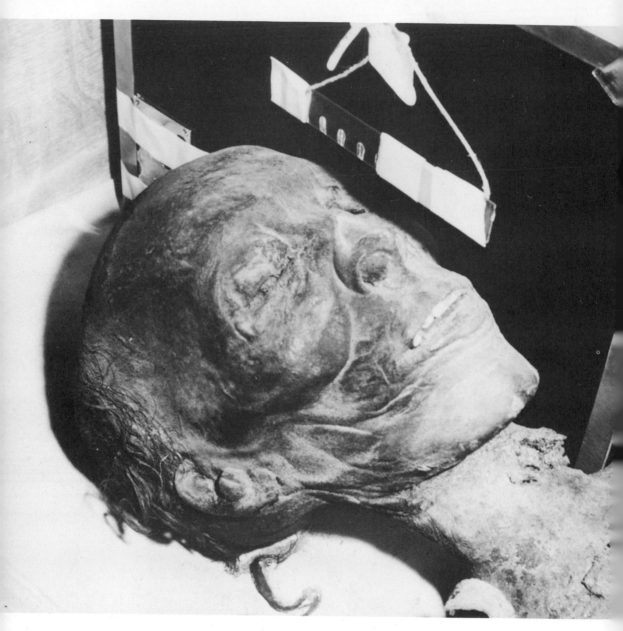

An x-ray cassette is placed next to the head of the mummy of Thutmosis
II in preparation for the exposure of a conventional lateral head plate.
The emaciated condition of the face suggests that this king, who died
at about thirty years of age, was a frail individual or had suffered from
disease for a long time before his death. The resemblance between Thutmosis I and Thutmosis II is readily apparent.

The mummy of the "elder woman" found in the tomb of Amenhotep II along with many royal mummies has been suggested by some scholars to be that of Queen Hatshepsut. The left hand is significant, since it is placed over the chest in the position observed in many pharaohs after Thutmosis I. Hatshepsut is known to have assumed the titles and role of pharaoh on the death of her husband, Thutmosis II (after G. Elliot Smith, "The Royal Mummies," *Catalogue Générale . . .*, Cairo, 1912, plate XCVII).

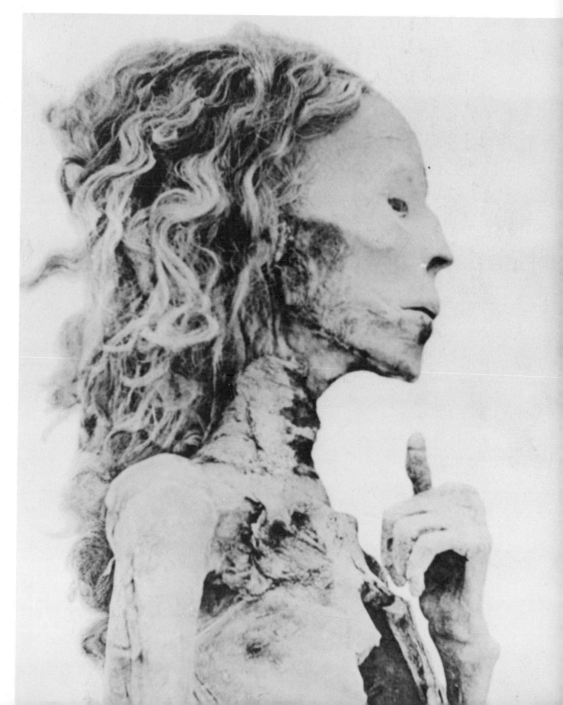

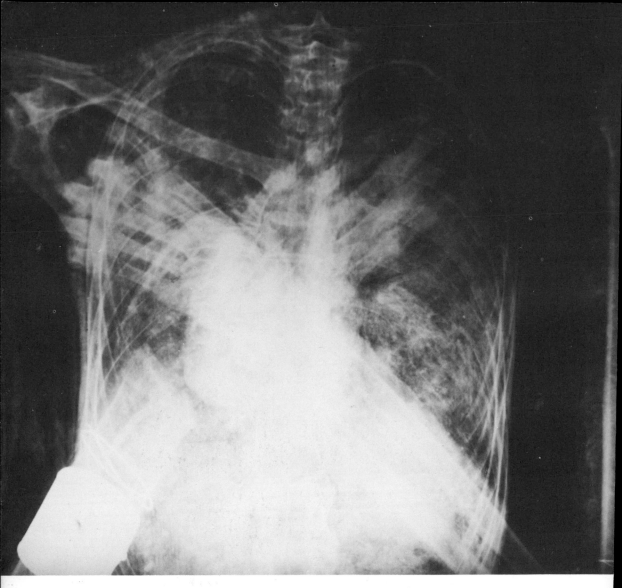

Thutmosis III, who assumed the throne at the death of Queen Hatshep-sut, was perhaps the greatest pharaoh of the New Kingdom. The x-rays of the chest area reveal his hands crossed on his chest and a wide metal bracelet on his right arm. The twisted wire was probably added later by the priests who sought to restore the badly damaged mummy.

The lateral head x-rays of Amenhotep II (OPPOSITE, TOP) and his son Thutmosis IV (BELOW) reveal a very close physical similarity in the jaws and the shapes of the skulls. Because the pharaohs as a group were so dissimilar, x-rays provide one of the few means of determining familial relationship.

38

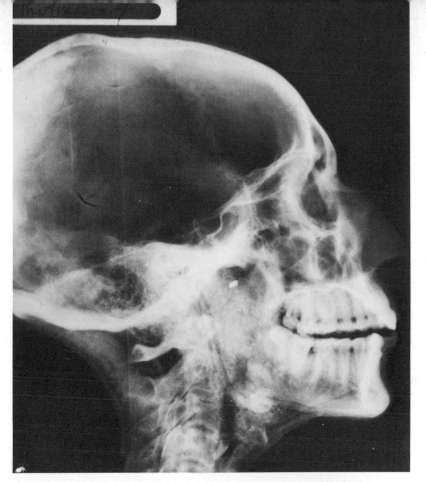
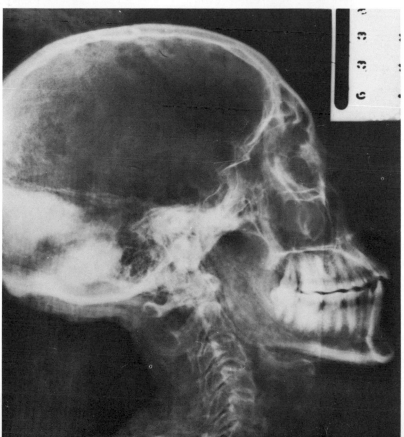

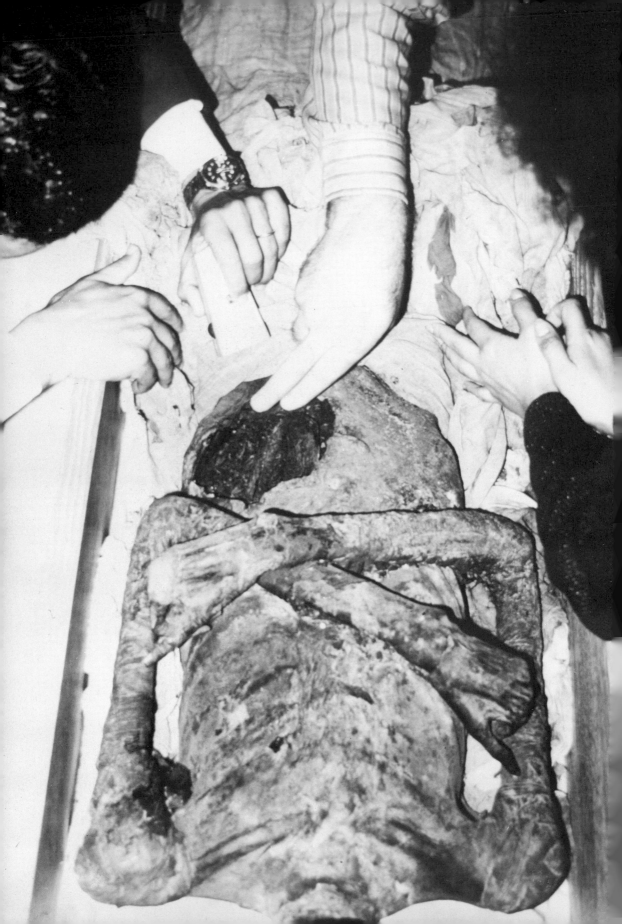

The crudely made embalming incision through which the viscera were removed for better preservation is clearly shown in the mummy of Thutmosis IV.

The mummies of Yuya and Thuya, the father and mother of Tiye, wife of Amenhotep III, are among the best-preserved in the Egyptian Museum (SEE COLORPLATES). Both have long flaxen hair, and stubble was evident on Yuya's face. When the linen wrappings were drawn back, the traditional gold plate placed over the embalming incision could be seen on Yuya's mummy. The beautiful decoration on the wrappings is made of cloth soaked in plaster and covered with fine goldleaf. The lateral x-ray of Thuya's head reveals a distinctive facial type and also indicates severe dental disease and many missing teeth.

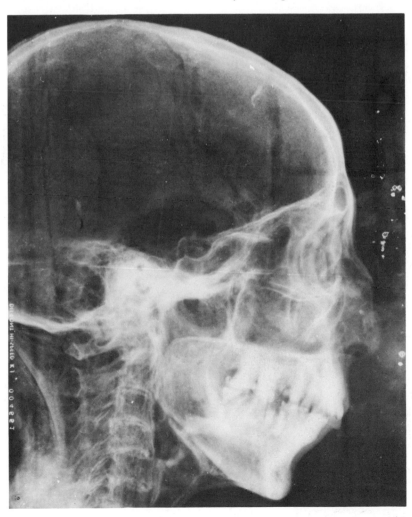

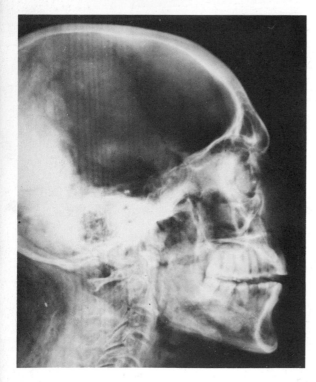

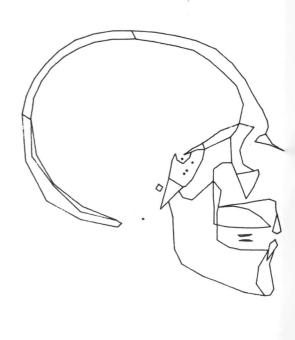

The mummy of Seti I is the most
lifelike of those of the great
pharaohs of Egypt, in spite of
the fact that the head was
broken from the body by grave
robbers (SEE ALSO
COLORPLATE). *Because of its
excellent preservation and the
distinctiveness of the facial
features, Seti I's mummy
(OPPOSITE, TOP LEFT) can be
compared with a relief of his
face on the Temple at Abydos
(TOP RIGHT). The lateral x-ray
of the mummy's head (BOTTOM
LEFT) was computerized
(BOTTOM RIGHT) so that it
could be compared with other
pharaohs by means of
mathematical analysis. In the
composite x-rays (RIGHT) of Seti
I, a funerary object, the sacred
Eye of Horus, may be observed
on the left arm. The Eye
remained undiscovered by grave
robbers or archaeologists, since it
lay beneath minor wrappings
and the body's resinous coating.*

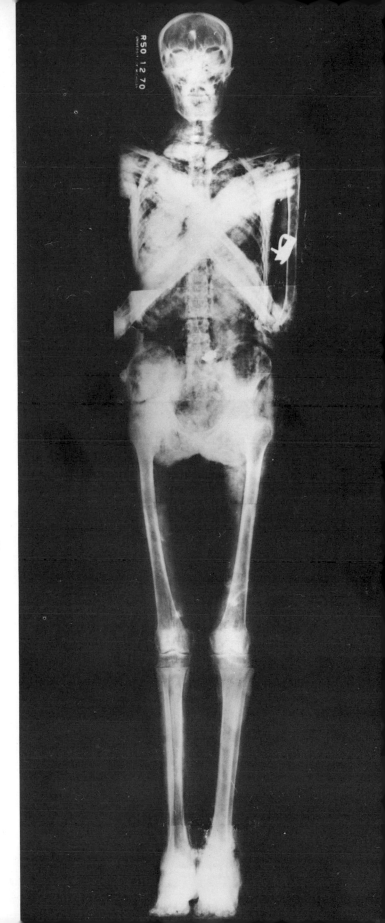

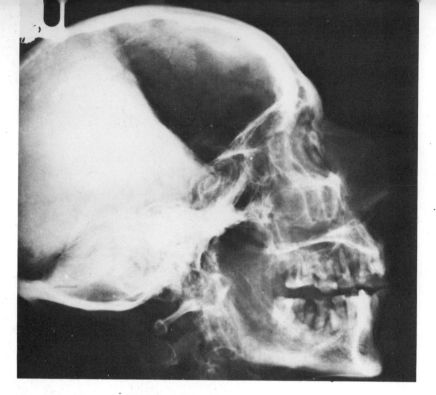

Ramesses II, son of Seti I and builder of the temple at Abu Simbel and many other great monuments of Egypt, was about seventy when he died. The extensive remodeling of the skull shown in the lateral x-ray reflects the aging process; extensive dental wear and abscesses are also evident.

The mummy of Merenptah, one of the many sons of Ramesses II, is of special interest because of the discoloration of the skin caused by salts (SEE COLORPLATE). Early writers speculated that this occurred because the pharaoh drowned in the sea during the Exodus, but this is not true. The process of mummification at that time often produced such discoloration. The lateral x-ray of Merenptah reveals that, like his father, he suffered greatly from dental problems; by the time of his death most of his back teeth were missing. The prominent nose appears to be characteristic of the kings of this period.

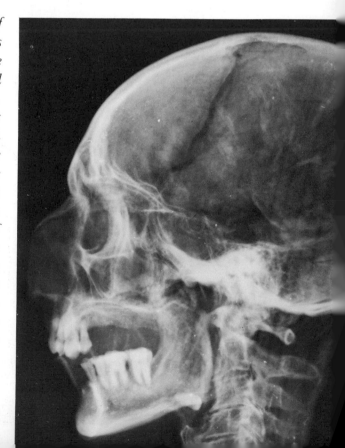

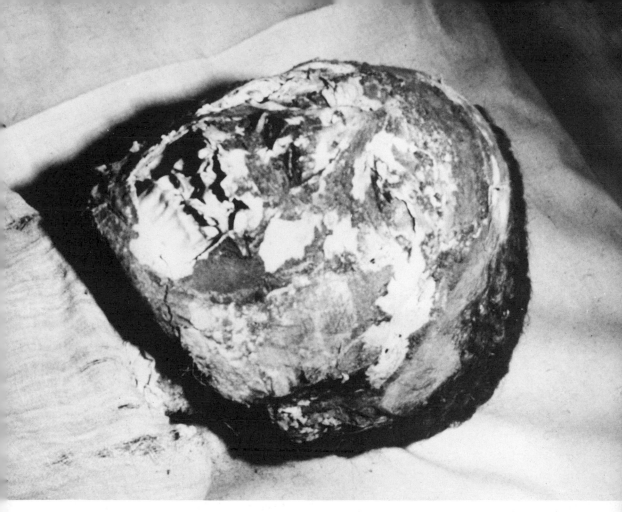

Grave robbers had done serious damage to the mummy of Siptah, the son of Seti II. The discoloration of the skin is similar to that in Merenptah's mummy. The x-rays of Siptah's feet revealed that one was deformed. In the past this condition has been described as a "club foot," but the x-rays suggest poliomyelitis as an alternative diagnosis.

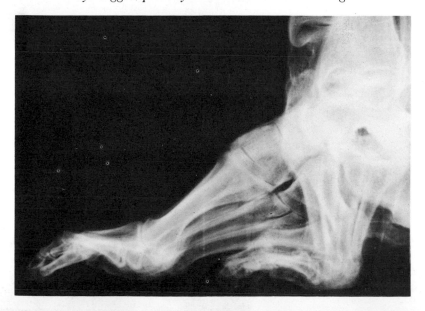

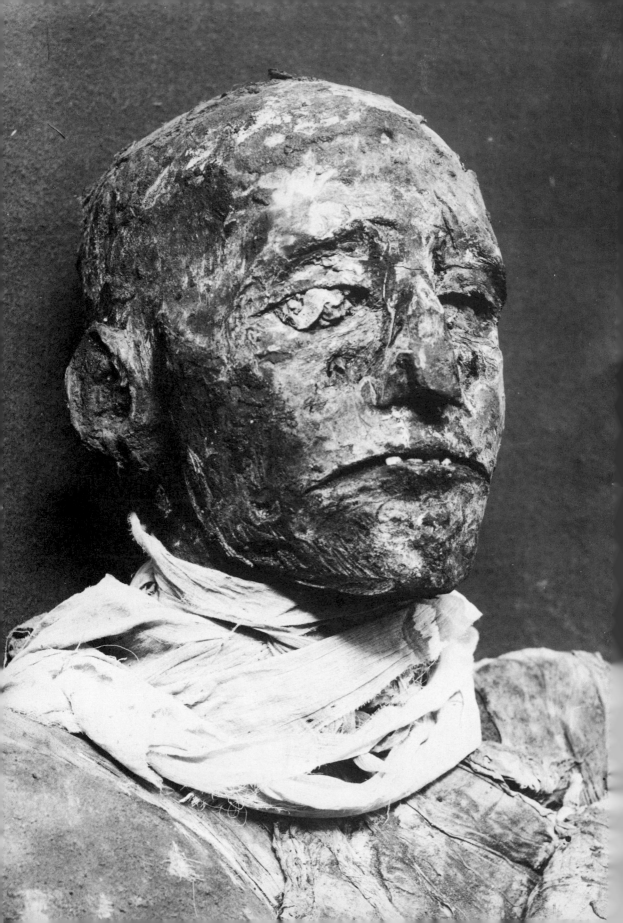

The well-preserved mummy of Ramesses III, which has provided the model for innumerable horror films, is especially interesting because of the packing of the eye sockets and the pierced ears; the latter was a common attribute of later Egyptian kings. In the lateral x-ray of this pharaoh's head, the opaque areas are the result of resins and other materials inserted into the brain case.

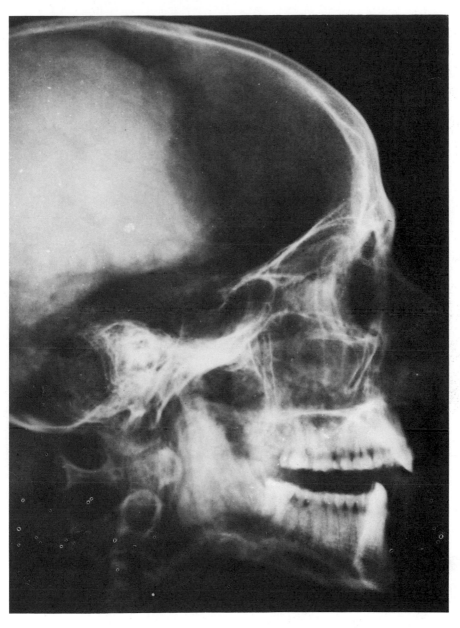

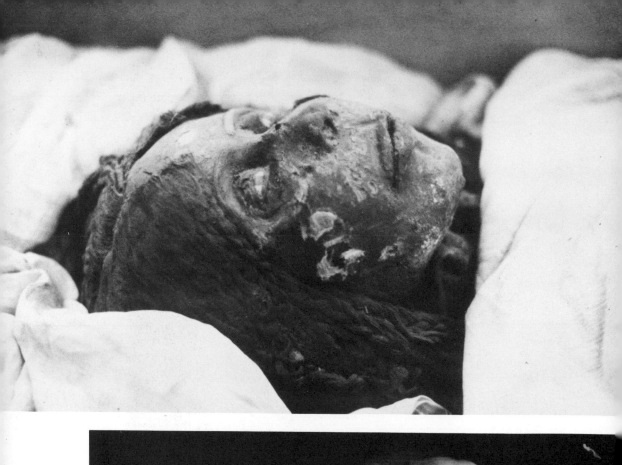
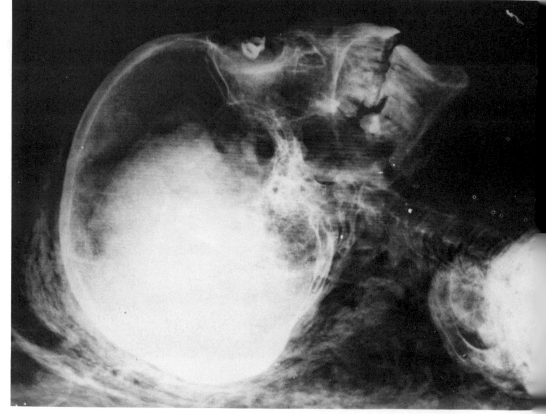

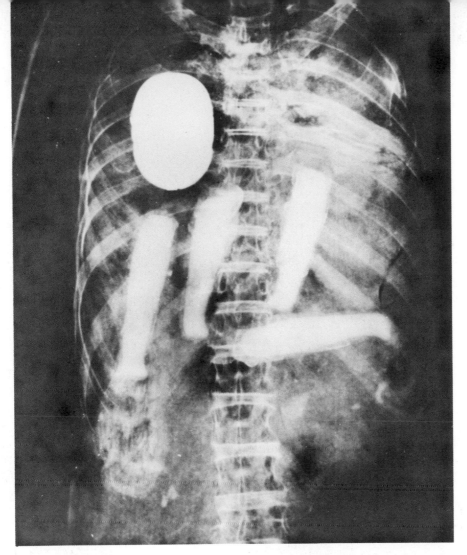

Embalming practices that resulted in an almost doll-like appearance are illustrated by the mummy of Queen Nodjme of the Twenty-first Dynasty (OPPOSITE, TOP). Braided hair, artificial eyes, and the packing of the cheeks and limbs are characteristic of a different approach to mummification after the Eighteenth Dynasty. The lateral x-ray of Nodjme's head (OPPOSITE, BOTTOM) reveals the artificial eyes placed in the sockets by the embalmers, as well as a rounded facial profile and dental protrusion, similar to other queens of this period. Numerous dental problems may be seen in the molar region. The frontal chest x-ray (ABOVE) of Nodjme shows small wax statuettes of the Four Sons of Horus and a large heart scarab lying on the right side. (The real heart is evident on the left; as the "seat of wisdom," it was never removed.) In the early years of the New Kingdom, the viscera were placed in jars representing the Four Sons of Horus; not until late in that period were the viscera usually returned to the body after it was preserved.

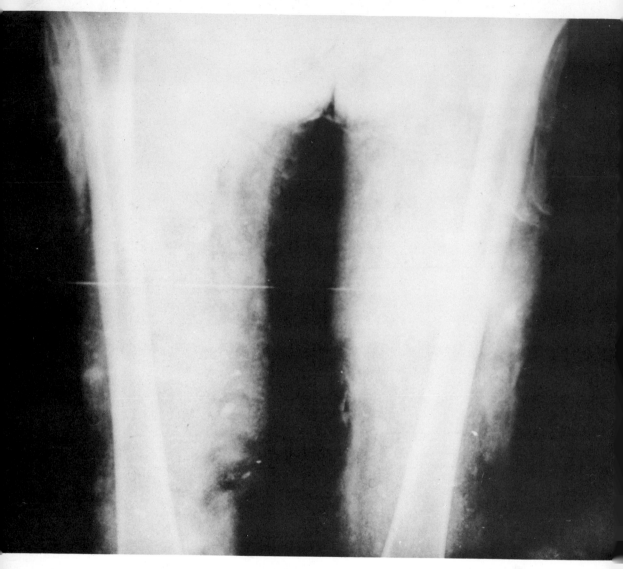

In the mummy of Queen Henttowy of the Twenty-first Dynasty excessive packing of the face to restore a lifelike appearance has caused the skin to burst (SEE COLORPLATE). The x-rays of Henttowy's legs also show heavy packing placed under the skin; such packing was an advance in technique by the embalmers of the time.

The mummy of Queen Esemkhebe, wife of Pinudjem II of the Twenty-first Dynasty, has not been unwrapped since it is an excellent example of the careful wrapping characteristic of this period.

50

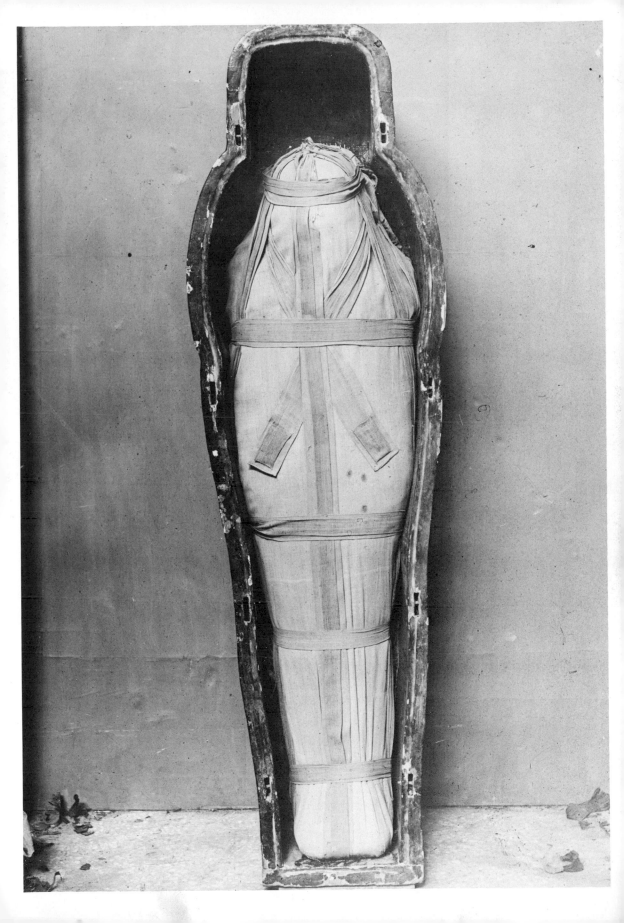

The funerary papyrus of Makare, a high priestess of Amon, shows her seated before a table of funerary offerings. A shawabti, a figure designed to serve her needs in the afterlife, stands behind her (from Naville, *Papyrus Funeraires de la XXIe Dynastie*, Paris, 1912, plate I).

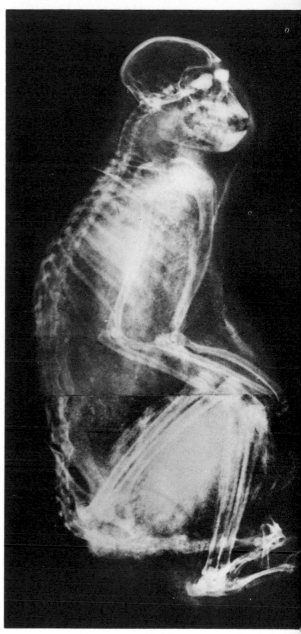

*The wrapped mummy (*LEFT*) found buried with Makare and originally labeled the Princess Moutemhet was found on x-ray examination to be that of a female hamadryas baboon (*RIGHT*). Since the mummy of Makare appears to be that of a woman who had recently delivered a child, this discovery has raised many questions.*

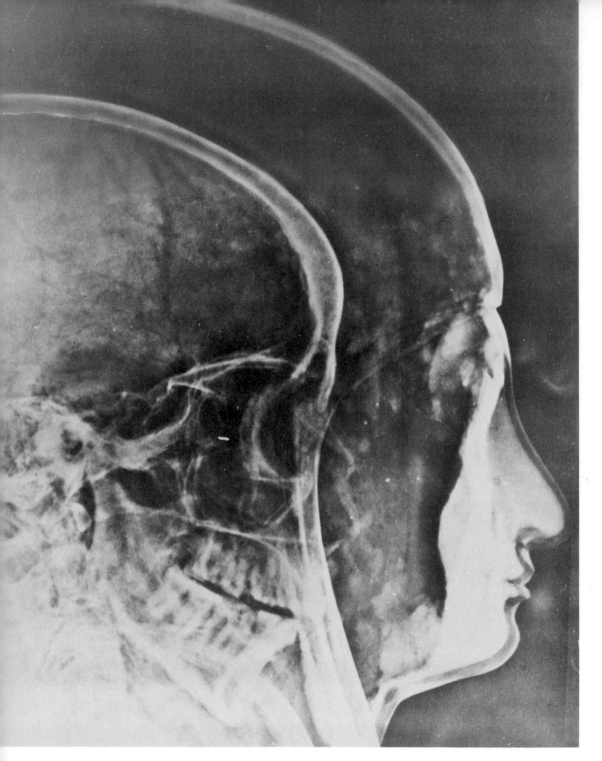

X-rays reveal the perfect integration between the face of the never-unwrapped mummy of Ta-pero, a court lady of the Twenty-second Dynasty, and her sarcophagus. At this time the art of mummification had reached perhaps its highest level.

X-RAYING
THE PHARAOHS

ONE  THE MUMMY
—Clue to the Past

No relic of antiquity has been more romanticized or made the subject of more incredible misinformation than have ancient Egyptian mummies. Visitors to the Mummy Room of the Egyptian Museum in Cairo often expect to see mummies as they appeared in the horror films of the 1930s: grotesque figures with fearsome grins and sunken eyes, bandages just loose enough to reveal a fist clenching nine tanna leaves, lying in gilt sarcophagi, waiting with sinister patience for the unwelcome intruder to stray too close.

Visitors with such expectations are invariably disappointed. Mummies look unreal, with their leatherlike skin and frozen features, but certainly not frightening, and they lie in simple oak coffins in a stark room that resembles a storeroom more than a repository for ancient royalty.

While the Hollywood version of Egyptian mummies is a figment of vivid imagination, and most of us realize that they are not terrifying creatures ready to invoke ancient curses, few are aware that mummies are worthwhile subjects of scholarly research. In fact, a number of Egyptologists and medical scientists have devoted their time to this study.

1.

Most people believe that since the hieroglyphs of ancient Egypt can be read, its art analyzed, its buildings excavated, a vividly clear picture of Egyptian life has been reconstructed. Unfortunately, this is not true. Egyptology is a young discipline—hieroglyphs could not be read accurately until well after Jean François Champollion published his decipherment in 1822—and most of the texts from ancient Egypt are still in need of careful translation. Scientific archaeology is even younger, and of the thousands of archaeological sites known in Egypt, the vast majority are still undug, or only partially dug, or destroyed by thieves and untrained amateurs. In fact, while a historical skeleton of ancient Egypt can be constructed, there is not much flesh to add to its bones. For the study of three aspects of ancient Egypt—anthropology, medicine, and mummification—only ancient mummies can be of help. Papyri, paintings, and texts simply do not tell enough.

The questions that a study of ancient mummies can help answer cover a wide range. From what diseases did the ancient Egyptians suffer? What surgical techniques did they use? How did diet affect their health? How long did they live? Where did they come from? How did they prepare their dead for burial? The remains of the Egyptians themselves can provide answers, and these answers can have great effect upon the very foundation of Egyptological study, the chronological framework upon which all other data are based.

The value of mummies for Egyptological study has been recognized since the late nineteenth century when two great caches of royal mummies were discovered at Thebes. Almost every known mummy of an Egyptian ruler comes from these two caches. Prior to their discovery, mummies had been looked upon simply as curiosities, and most had not even been recorded or saved by excavators.

The interest stirred by the royal mummies after they had been moved from Thebes to the Egyptian Museum caused two scholars to attempt systematic examinations of the collection. The first was by the French Egyptologist Gaston Maspero in 1889; the second, in 1912, by the English anatomist Grafton Elliot Smith.

Any complete examination of mummified remains requires that the bodies be unwrapped and their internal structures probed and analyzed. While an occasional mummy had been dissected and a full-scale autopsy performed in Europe or America, neither Maspero nor Smith felt that the royal mummies could be so treated. These mummies formed, after all, a unique collection. Many of them were so beautifully wrapped that to destroy their bandages and dissect their organs was unthinkable. For a number of the royal mummies, therefore, Maspero and Smith had to rely solely upon superficial examination. Needless to say, they learned little about the physical attributes of these early Egyptian rulers. Their studies posed many questions but provided only few answers.

The development of the x-ray by the German physicist Wilhelm Konrad Roentgen in 1895 was, of course, a boon for the non-destructive study of ancient mummies.

However, the costly and cumbersome equipment required at this early stage of its development made it nearly impossible to use x-rays on any but a very few mummies. Smith wrote in the preface of his 1912 report: "Examination with the aid of x-rays would, no doubt, have provided much additional information—and I hope that this will be done at some future time—but I was unable to get such investigations carried out, except in the case of the mummy of Thoutmosis IV."[1]

It was not until December 1966, when an x-ray unit of sufficient portability had been designed and a staff of qualified scientists assembled, that the Egyptian Museum collection could be examined. Only then were the internal features of the wrapped mummies, inaccessible to Maspero and Smith, exposed for analysis.

2.

The project to x-ray the pharaohs came about not directly because of Egyptological interest but because a group of dentists at the University of Michigan's School of Dentistry was curious about the way in which human dentition has evolved over the past several thousand years and to this end was studying the people of a long-neglected land called Nubia.

Lying in the southernmost part of Egypt, and extending south along the Nile into the Sudan, Nubia has been a major crossroads of civilizations for over four thousand years. Its barren, sand-covered slopes have been occupied by the peoples and cultures of dynastic Egypt, of Africa, Greece, Rome, and even Europe, and it has absorbed and adopted as its own many different cultural attributes. Yet until recently very little has been known of Nubia's early history and development. Few written records dealing with Nubia have survived; of these, some are in languages we cannot yet translate. Archaeologists, who might have added much information through excavation, have generally chosen to work downstream on the more impressive remains of ancient Egypt.

When in 1960 President Gamal Abdel Nasser of Egypt announced the construction of the Aswan High Dam, which lies on the border between Nubia and what in ancient times was called Egypt, an urgent appeal was made to scholars to record as much as possible of this land before the rising floodwaters destroyed and buried it forever.

Most of those who answered his appeal concerned themselves with tracing ancient Nubian village and temple plans, reconstructing its economy and religion, plotting variations in its pottery styles. Such studies yielded a wealth of information about how these people lived nearly two millennia ago. A few projects were also concerned with the ancient Nubians themselves, analyzing their skeletons and the desiccated remains of their dead in the hope of learning more about who these people were, how they died, and from what diseases they might have suffered during their lifetime.

In 1965 Kent R. Weeks, an American scholar now on the staff of the American University in Cairo, went to the Nubian site of Gebel Adda, about seven hundred miles south of Cairo, near the Temple of Abu Simbel, to study skeletons being excavated by the American Research Center in Egypt. Under the direction of Nicholas Millet, an American Egyptologist, that expedition had been excavating an elaborate townsite and seven huge cemeteries, from which they had recovered and saved over five thousand skeletons and naturally desiccated bodies, one of the largest collections of human remains ever made available from a single site. In the strictest sense, the bodies at Gebel Adda were not mummies but simply human remains that had been desiccated and preserved naturally by the heat and dryness of the sand in which they had been buried. To be a mummy, the body would have had to have been deliberately treated with certain specific embalming techniques.

The skeletons spanned a period from about the time of the birth of Christ to the eighteenth century A.D. Because of the many incursions of foreigners into Nubia, they offered the possibility of testing new anthropological techniques designed to identify changes in the genetic composition of a population. The soft tissue of the bodies—the desert heat had dried out the tissue but had not destroyed it—provided samples for the study of pathological conditions and an opportunity to see if mathematical methods of determining sex from skeletons were accurate.

Weeks and his assistant carefully made a series of 149 measurements on each of these skeletons and bodies, photographed them, described their abnormalities, and took hundreds of bone and tissue samples for later laboratory analysis. But it rapidly became clear that if the population, past and present, was to be analyzed with the detail necessary to show physical changes and the effects of diet and environment upon health, considerably more attention would have to be paid to Nubian teeth.

Why teeth? There are several reasons. First, teeth are among the best and most commonly preserved parts of the human body, which means that large samples from a number of different areas and periods are available for comparative study. Second, dentition provides an excellent gauge of the effects of environment on the human body and reflects human variation and disorders of a hereditary nature. Third, dentition and the bones of the face form one of the most often discussed biological complexes in the body, a complex of considerable concern and one about which very little is known.

Dentition offers such wide-ranging possibilities for analysis that considerable time is needed for its study. To perform the kind of dental study a sample as large as that of Gebel Adda demanded, a full-scale expedition was necessary. James E. Harris of the University of Michigan, a geneticist and orthodontist interested in the dentition of ancient man, was asked to direct this project, and in 1965 he assembled a staff and made the ten-thousand-mile journey from Michigan to Gebel Adda.

For a number of years Harris and his colleagues had been studying the ways in which orthodontists (dentists concerned with dental alignment and facial growth) might better predict the pattern of development of human dentition. Since everyone has a set of teeth that has been influenced both by personal history and by genetic ancestry, the successful treatment of any errors in dental growth, such as malocclusion (popularly called buck teeth), depends upon the careful analysis not only of the individual but of his ancestry and of the population of which he is a part. Nearly half of all children born have teeth that are severely enough maloccluded to require some correction. How can an orthodontist determine whether badly overcrowded teeth require braces, extraction, surgery, or nothing but time to be corrected? Until recently he would have had to rely upon educated guesswork.

A few years before coming to Egypt, Harris had conducted a study of schoolchildren in Michigan to determine what role age, family dental history, population trends, and genetic factors played in facial growth. From this study he was able to add a high degree of predictability to orthodontic treatment. The more accurately an orthodontist can predict how a child's face will grow, the more accurately he can correct any errors in development of occlusion (dental bite).

To test and refine his theories, Harris needed to study a population that would allow him not only to follow an individual's dental development over a number of years, but to compare individuals of the same population over several centuries. Dental records in America did not go back far enough to allow such a study, and the heterogeneity of America's population, the genetic mixing of a number of formerly isolated groups, meant that so many variables were present in the population that no real conclusions could be drawn.

Nubia was the logical place for Harris's study. The Gebel Adda material offered a large collection of human remains spanning nearly two thousand years, and the contemporary descendants of these early inhabitants, living in new villages near Aswan, provided the continuity for determining dental evolution. In spite of the many foreign incursions the group as a whole has remained remarkably homogeneous; thus the confusing picture presented by heterogeneous American and European populations would not be an obstacle here.

These population features proved important. Crowding, for example, a dental condition in which the teeth are too close together or too far apart, is thought to be due to man's jaws having become increasingly smaller as he has evolved, while his teeth have remained nearer the same size. The project found evidence to support this theory. Harris was able to demonstrate that modern Nubians have smaller faces, smaller jaws, and more crowding of the teeth than their ancestors did. Among contemporary Nubian schoolchildren the effects of this process could clearly be seen because their poor diet resulted in slowed bone growth, while their permanent teeth erupted at an earlier age than among American children.

Buck teeth, called Class II malocclusions by orthodontists, are common in the United States but rare in Egypt, and the size of the Nubian sample made it possible to determine the extent to which such acquired habits as thumb-sucking and tongue-thrusting forced the teeth forward and the extent to which the problem was genetic in origin. Harris found that such Class II malocclusions among Nubians occurred only among those children who also had acquired habits that put abnormal pressure on their front teeth.

Harris's team worked at Gebel Adda during the late spring of 1965 and among the living Nubians at Aswan during the four subsequent years. Almost one thousand skulls were x-rayed at Gebel Adda, over two thousand schoolchildren studied at Aswan.

One aspect of the Nubian project that was of particular interest to the dentists was the effect of diet upon the growth and health of teeth. In the past, as the Gebel Adda collection showed, the major dental problems in Nubia were caused by the heavy wear to which the teeth were subjected. Coarse foods and quantities of sand that infiltrated almost everything quickly wore teeth down almost to the gum line. Caries, on the other hand, were uncommon. It was the heavy wear that exposed the interior of the tooth, bringing with it infection and often resulting in the death of the pulp.

With their move to new villages near Aswan to escape the rising waters of the Nile, the Nubians have been introduced to a different kind of diet, which has already had its effects upon Nubian dentition. This changed diet, which is still being studied by the Michigan Expedition, contains less sand, more refined food, and great quantities of sugar from the nearby sugar-cane fields. The Nubians are now beginning to experience the dental caries from which people in the West have suffered so badly for centuries.

3.

One aspect of the effect of diet on dentition, particularly in earlier times, could not be examined among either the Gebel Adda remains or the living Nubians. This was the possible relationship between dentition and social class. It seems logical to expect that members of the upper social classes in ancient Egypt would have suffered dental problems different from those of the peasants because their diet would presumably have been richer and more varied. To test this idea, which might have important consequences for the study of ancient Egyptian society, it was necessary to analyze the dentition of people definitely known to have been members of the upper economic class and to compare this with the dentition of members of a known lower economic class.

The Nubians were a good starting point for the study of the lower economic classes and, indeed, their skeletons were the only large sample of such a class from Egypt. Farther north, the cemeteries of commoners of dynastic times have not survived.

When the Nubian study was completed, it was necessary to find samples of "upper-class" mummies. With the permission of the Egyptian Antiquities Department, the Michigan Expedition began an x-ray study of a number of mummies and skeletons from the collection at Giza, dating from the Old Kingdom and known to include members of ancient Egypt's official class; and from a smaller collection of New Kingdom date at Thebes, also consisting of officials and lesser nobility.

After completing the work at Giza and Thebes, permission was sought to x-ray the unique and highly important collection of royal mummies, spanning the broadest range of Egypt's history, which were exhibited in the Egyptian Museum. The museum was interested in this plan—these mummies had still not been completely studied—for it promised a great deal of information, not only on diet and social class in relation to dental health, but on a number of other important questions that were perplexing Egyptologists.

Both the members of the Michigan Expedition and the museum staff had very high hopes as the equipment was moved from Aswan to Cairo. Work was begun one morning in December 1966 by the first of the expeditions to the Egyptian Museum.

The expedition was confronted by two problems that first season. There was only a short time left after the problems of moving equipment from Aswan, and only frontal and lateral x-rays of the pharaohs' heads were obtained. Head-to-toe x-rays would have been preferable, since many of the mummies had never been unwrapped and held the possibility of revealing pathological conditions and, perhaps, artifacts.

More important, the museum staff was justifiably concerned about the mummies, which, after three thousand years, were in fragile condition, and they asked that the x-raying be done through the glass display cases and no attempt be made to move the mummies about. This added greatly to the exposure time necessary to obtain prints, and, after several tests, it was discovered that the glass used in the cases was leaded. The x-rays penetrated, with three- to five-minute exposures, but the resulting prints were generally foggy and lacking detail.

In spite of the rather poor quality of the prints, everything went smoothly. The members of the expedition did not disrupt the work of the museum, nothing was damaged, and even the foggy x-rays proved interesting. The director of the museum, Henry Riad, realizing the problems the leaded glass cases had caused, and pleased with the results, invited the expedition to return the following year, when, he promised, the cases could be opened and clearer x-rays made.

For that second season we changed x-ray machines. Instead of the easily portable unit used in Nubia, which operated on radioactive Ytterbium 169, a larger but still portable machine, similar to those in dental offices, was used. The problems posed during the first season—long exposure time, difficulty in maintaining a proper scale on the x-rays, and having to shoot through the leaded glass—were all solved.

We arrived at the museum each morning at nine o'clock and, after signing the guard's register, proceeded upstairs to Gallery 52 where the mummies were displayed. While some of the staff began the task of setting the x-ray unit on its tripod, adjusting the transformers, and loading the film cassettes, two of us would decide on the mummies to be x-rayed that day. After a museum official and a guard arrived to oversee the work, the museum riggers would take one of the huge display cases, slide it into a narrow passage in the crowded room, and remove the leaded glass lid. Inside, the pharaoh lay in a solid oak coffin, covered with linen. Gingerly the workmen would carry the surprisingly heavy coffin to the x-ray machine. Then the difficult job began.

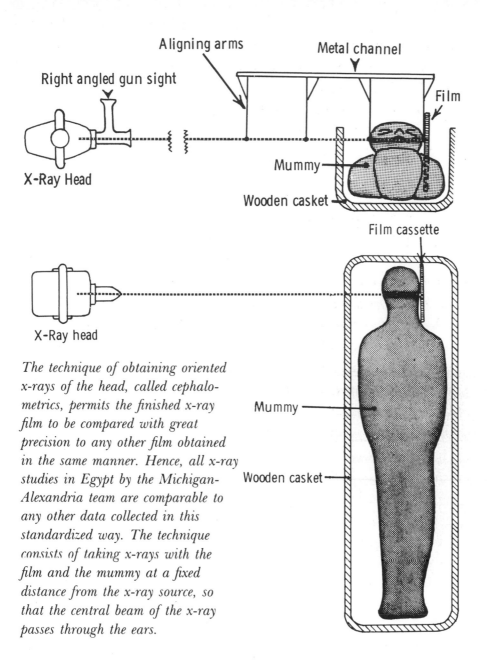

Aligning arms

Metal channel

Right angled gun sight

Film

X-Ray Head

Mummy

Wooden casket

Film cassette

X-Ray head

Mummy

Wooden casket

The technique of obtaining oriented x-rays of the head, called cephalometrics, permits the finished x-ray film to be compared with great precision to any other film obtained in the same manner. Hence, all x-ray studies in Egypt by the Michigan-Alexandria team are comparable to any other data collected in this standardized way. The technique consists of taking x-rays with the film and the mummy at a fixed distance from the x-ray source, so that the central beam of the x-ray passes through the ears.

To insure that each x-ray would exactly match the others in the series, the mummy had to be carefully aligned in the x-ray unit to prevent any possible distortion. Some of the pharaohs lay in their coffins with heads down or twisted out of line, and these had to be moved delicately until they exactly matched a series of points in the alignment unit. Too much moving, too sudden a jolt, and the mummy's skin might crumble or a bone snap, and it often took the steady hands of four men half an hour to position the body.

The x-rays were taken, usually six to eight of each mummy, and the films rushed to a makeshift darkroom in a nearby hotel for developing. If they were acceptable, the workmen carefully returned the mummy to its case, sealed it, and prepared to bring another pharaoh to the unit. It was slow work, and the average was four mummies a day. Easy though this process may sound, we all watched nervously as each mummy was carried across the room. One slip and our expedition would have been responsible for the destruction of an invaluable and irreplaceable archaeological legacy.

During the third season a complete set of head-to-toe x-rays of each of the royal mummies was obtained. Some revealed important material for physicians and Egyptologists—information on pathological conditions, artifacts, and unusual techniques of mummification.

The museum staff, impressed with the data revealed by the x-rays, informed us that there was a large number of other mummies in the museum, stored in the attic, all of them wrapped, in good condition, and largely unstudied. We were asked to return for a fourth season, and the following year we again set up our x-ray machine in the museum.

One member of the museum staff told us that the attic storeroom had been locked for as long as he could remember—thirty years or more, he said. Stepping over the threshold into two inches of choking dust, we felt like excavators entering a tomb that had been sealed for millennia. The small attic room was filled with sarcophagi, stacked three deep along the walls, like some ancient embalmer's storeroom. There were nearly forty mummies of the late New Kingdom, high priests, officials, and others, all named and in excellent condition. It took two seasons to complete the x-rays of this fascinating group, most of which were so well wrapped that Smith, in his 1912 study, had been able to describe them only cursorily.

In five seasons of work at the Egyptian Museum, all but two or three of the mummies in its possession were x-rayed. But the goal of the expedition was not simply to collect x-rays of each of the mummies in the museum. In our Ann Arbor laboratory, anthropologists, statisticians, orthodontists, and technicians have been kept busy for the past five years analyzing the x-rays of the ancient kings, comparing them to the x-rays from Nubia, Giza, and Thebes, trying to learn more about the anthropology and health of ancient Egypt.

The relationships among the pharaohs are a particularly challenging problem, one that cannot be solved simply by visually comparing two x-rays. A great number of factors have to be taken into account, particularly measurable morphological relationships between parts of the skull, and this requires that the x-rays be converted to an accurate series of mathematical comparisons. A highly complex computer program, designed a few years ago for the study of cranio-facial growth, was used to accomplish this task quickly and accurately.[2]

On a cranial x-ray, a series of points are spotted in much the same way that points on a map are plotted, using a series of coordinates. These points and the relationships between them are automatically fed to a computer through an "x-y digital coordinate system." Using these data, the computer "draws" a schematic figure of the skull with each of the 177 points mathematically defined. From such figures and the resulting statistical output of the computer program, skulls can be compared with an extremely high degree of accuracy. These computerized tracings are also useful in the study of the ancient representations of the pharaohs in sculpture and tomb paintings.

From the x-rays and laboratory analyses much has been learned about Egypt's ancient population. One of the most interesting conclusions, one of great importance to Egyptologists, is that the pharaohs as a whole form an extremely heterogeneous group. Indeed, if it were not known that all of these mummies were of Egyptian kings, if they had been found in different parts of the world, for example, no one would have assumed any relationship among them.

TWO ☥ THE MAKING OF THE MUMMY
—*Preparation for Eternity*

Of all the artifacts of ancient Egyptian culture, none is more fascinating than the mummy. It is still commonly believed that the techniques of mummification remain a mystery, that they evaded the inquiring scientist and died with the Egyptians when their civilization collapsed. This is not true. Since the time of ancient Greece these techniques have been examined and described by travelers; and since the eighteenth century, when Europeans diligently scoured the Nile Valley for a souvenir mummy to display in their homes, scores of physicians, chemists, historians, and curious tourists have analyzed mummified remains to learn more of this ancient art.

One of the most frequently asked questions about ancient Egypt is: What exactly are mummies? To answer this, some knowledge of the culture in which they were developed as well as the techniques of preparing them is necessary.

1.

The history of dynastic Egypt began about 3200 B.C. when two very different groups of people—one living in in the marshy delta of Lower Egypt, the other living along the Nile from what is now Cairo south to Aswan (Upper Egypt)—were united under a single government. Nothing is known of how Narmer, the king reputed to have engineered this unification, achieved his goal, but in a matter of only a few decades the Two Lands, Upper and Lower Egypt, became the economic and cultural focus of the ancient world.

The civilization of ancient Egypt survived for nearly three thousand years. During this time Egypt achieved great heights of power and cultural achievement in the periods called the Old, Middle, and New Kingdoms, and fell to near collapse during three intervening Intermediate Periods, when famine or foreigners invaded the country.

The first flowering of Egyptian culture occurred a few centuries after the unification, in the period of the Old Kingdom (Third Dynasty through Eighth Dynasty), from about 2700 B.C. to 2150 B.C. The sphinx at Giza and nearly fifty pyramids are visible examples of its achievements. An efficient system of agriculture made possible the leisure time necessary for the development of a literate class of specialists, freed from the necessity of tending the fields, able to devote itself to science and arts. Geometry, engineering, medicine, and religion advanced rapidly. The government, uninterested in territorial expansion and well protected by the natural barriers of desert and sea, encouraged cultural growth.

A superb art was developed, as shown by the elegantly

THE MAKING OF THE MUMMY

carved and painted reliefs found on the walls of tombs built near the capital, Memphis, only a few miles from modern Cairo. These were not the dull and formal scenes of man meeting his god at the gates of heaven, but bright, happy pictures of fishing, banquets, hunting, and sports; gentle scenes of a man and his wife chatting with their children; scenes that reflected the Egyptian's greatest wish: that even after death the pleasant and desirable things of life—the beauty of the Nile and the desert, the peace of a happy home—might always be enjoyed.

Contrary to modern belief, the people of ancient Egypt were not morbid souls who constantly meditated on death. They recognized death, of course, but for them it was not the final, absolute end. Rather, it was the continuation of life in a different form. What they enjoyed and found pleasant in this life they tried to take with them into the next. To insure this, techniques of mummification were developed.

The first examples extant date from the Old Kingdom, but mummification of a sort had been practiced long before this time. The simple agriculturalists of the Nile Valley had already developed a belief in the afterlife, which formed the foundation upon which later Egyptian religion was to build.

These ancestors of dynastic Egypt had buried their dead in shallow desert graves, wrapping them in sheets of linen or hides or mats, drawing the knees up under the chin in a close approximation of the fetal position. In the hot sand a natural drying of the body took place, leaving soft tissues in a well-preserved state, with the appearance of old leather. This natural desiccation, and hence preservation, of the body was not nearly so effective when the Egyptians began building tomb chambers deep in the ground, where the body was not protected by the hot dry sand. It may have been this change in burial practice that inspired the development of artificial techniques for preparing the dead, so that all bodies might be preserved and retain a lifelike appearance.

Perhaps it was at this same time that Egyptians began to emphasize the religious beliefs that virtually demanded that such preservation be attempted. In dynastic Egypt it was believed that a man was protected during his life by three spiritual elements, only one of which abandoned his body after death. Two of them, the *ka* and the *ba*, remained.

The *ka* was a man's double: it was born with him, embodied his qualities and characteristics, and after death resided with him in his tomb. The *ba*, perhaps similar to our "soul," traveled after death with the sun on its nightly journey through the underworld but returned to visit the deceased each morning. To the Egyptians these spiritual elements were not abstract, disembodied ghosts; they were real entities, and they required a place in which to dwell for eternity. The most appropriate dwelling place was the body of the deceased himself.

These two factors—the observation that bodies could be preserved and the belief that the *ka* and the *ba* required a tangible form in which to dwell—may very well have prompted the first attempts at mummification. The *ka* and the *ba* needed a home for eternity; thus the body had to be preserved for eternity. The soul had to be able to identify the body with which it was associated, and thus the body had to be molded into a lifelike form the spirits might recognize. The spirits had to have sustenance, and thus offerings of food had to be placed in the tomb. Destruction of the body or the loss of the food offerings (either real food or representations of food in relief scenes) would have meant the destruction of a man's soul and the loss of immortality.

As time passed, the techniques of mummification became more and more elaborate, for the Egyptians tried to insure the complete preservation of their dead. It was an expensive and time-consuming process, at first one only the royal family could afford. By the time of the New Kingdom, officials too were mummified, and toward the end of the dynastic period even members of the poorer classes could have their dead treated in this manner.

 2.

In the fifth century B.C., the Greek historian Herodotus visited Egypt and described how this mysterious craft was practiced. Although he was wrong in some details, his account of mummification has been one of the major sources for its study.

> There are a set of men who practise that art and make it their business. These persons, when a body is brought to them, show the bearers wooden models of corpses, painted so as to resemble nature. The most perfect they say to be after the manner of Him whom I do not think it religious to name in connection with such a matter; they then show the second kind, which is inferior to the first and less costly; then the third which is the cheapest. All this the embalmers explain, and then ask in which way it is wished that the corpse should be prepared. The bearers, having agreed on the price, take their departure. The embalmers remain in their workshop, and this is their procedure for the most perfect embalming. First, by the means of an iron hook, they

draw out the brain through the nostrils, taking it partly in this manner, partly by the infusion of drugs. Then with a sharp Ethiopian stone they make a cut along the whole contents of the abdomen, which they then cleanse, rinse with palm wine and rinse again with powdered aromatics. Then, having filled the belly with pure myrrh powdered, and cassia and every other kind of spicery except frankincense, they sew it up again. Having done this, they "cure" the body, leaving it covered with natron for seventy days; it is forbidden to "cure" it for a longer space of time. At the expiration of the seventy days they wash the corpse and wrap the whole body in bandages of linen cloth, smeared over with gum, which the Egyptians commonly use in place of glue. After this the relatives, having taken the body back again, have a wooden case made in the shape of a man and, when it is ready, enclose the body in it. They fasten the case and store it thus in a sepulchral chamber, upright against one of the walls. Such is the most costly way of preparing the corpse.

When the middle style is chosen and great expense is to be avoided, they prepare the corpse in the following manner. They charge their syringes with oil from cedar and fill with it the abdomen of the corpse, without making any incision or taking out the bowels; they inject the oil at the fundaments and, having prevented the injection from escaping, they "cure" the body for the prescribed number of days, and on the last day they let out from the abdomen the oil of cedar they had previously injected; such is the power of the oil that it brings with it the bowels and the flesh, and nothing remains of the body but the skin and the bones. Having done this, they return the body without further operation.

The third method of embalming is the following, which is practised in the case of the poorer classes: after clearing the abdomen with a purgative, they "cure" the body for the seventy days and deliver it to be carried.[1]

While Herodotus, like many modern tourists, was often prey to the exaggerated and erroneous tales told by local guides, his description has been confirmed in the writings of a later Greek historian, Diodorus Siculus, who visited Egypt four hundred years later, in the first century B.C. Compared to Herodotus, this later writer seems less clinical in his approach.

When a person amongst them dies, all his relatives and friends, putting mud upon their heads, go about the town lamenting, until the time of burying the body. In the meantime they abstain from bathing and from wine and all kinds of delicacies, neither do they wear fine apparel. They have three manners of burial: one very costly, one medium and one modest. Upon the first a talent of silver is spent, upon the second twenty monœ, but in the third there is very little cost. Those who attend to the bodies have learned their art from their forefathers. These, carrying to the household of the deceased illustrations of the costs of burial of each kind, ask them in which manner they desire the body to be treated. When all this is agreed upon, and the corpse is handed over, they [the relatives] deliver the body to those who are appointed to deal with it in the accustomed manner.

First he who is called the scribe, laying the body

down, marks on the left flank where it is to be cut. Then he who is called the cutter takes an ethiopian stone, and cuts the flesh as the law prescribes, and forthwith escapes running, those who are present pursuing and throwing stones and cursing the defilement [his act of cutting] on to his head. For whosoever inflicts violence upon, or wounds, or in any way injures a body of his own kind, they hold worthy hatred. The embalmers, on the other hand, they esteem worthy of every honour and respect, associating with the priests and being admitted to temples without hindrance as holy men. When they have assembled for the treatment of the body which has been cut, one of them inserts his hand through the wound in the corpse into the breast and takes out everything excepting the kidneys and heart. Another man cleanses each of the entrails, sweetening them with palm-wine and with incense. Finally, having washed the whole body, they first diligently treat it with cedar oil and other things for over thirty days, and then with myrrh and cinnamon and [spices] which not only have the power to preserve it for a long time, but also impart a fragrant smell. Having treated it, they restore it to the relatives with every member of the body preserved so perfectly that even the eyelashes and eyebrows remain, the whole appearance of the body being unchangeable, and the cast of the features recognisable. Therefore, many of the Egyptians keeping the bodies of their ancestors in fine chambers, can behold at a glance those who died before they themselves were born. Thus, while they contemplate the size and proportions of their bodies, and the very lineament of their faces, they present an example of a kind of inverted

THE MAKING OF THE MUMMY

necromancy and seem to live in the same age with those upon whom they look.[2]

Even to his own children, the mummified remains of the deceased seemed lifelike. But such elaborate techniques belong to a very late period of ancient Egypt, as far removed in time from the Old Kingdom as they are from us. To trace the process by which they came about, let us return to that earlier period.

3.

Attempts to preserve the body began simply enough during the first two dynasties. The body was wrapped tightly with strips of bandage; in some instances each limb was bound separately and then covered with larger sheets. For further protection, the body was placed in a wooden coffin. By the Third Dynasty it had become clear that these attempts were insufficient to insure a lasting home for the soul. The body still decomposed, the coffin rotted, and only bare bones remained. The use of stone sarcophagi instead of wooden ones proved of no help. The solution was to remove the most easily destroyed parts of the body, the internal organs, through a small incision in the abdomen, cleanse the cavity, and pack it with linen (the brain was not removed until later in Egyptian history). To preserve the external features, parts of the face and the genitals were molded in strips of linen soaked in an adhesive and placed inside the wrappings. Such reconstruction of the face would help the soul to recognize the body even if minor damage had occurred. The organs that had been removed were separately wrapped and placed in stone vessels, called "canopic jars," set near the body.

The most important objective of the mummification process was to remove from the body any liquids that might hasten decomposition. To be preserved, the body had in a sense to be dehydrated. During the Old Kingdom a substance called "natron" was found to promote this dehydration process.

Called by the ancient Egyptians *netjery* (from which the Greek word *nitron* and the chemical symbol for sodium, "Na," are derived), natron is a naturally occurring substance composed of sodium bicarbonate and sodium chloride (or sodium sulphate). It is found in three sites in Egypt, the best known of which is Wadi el-Natrun, about forty miles west of Cairo in the Libyan Desert. Before the building of dams and barrages on the Nile, the annual river flood raised the water table in this valley, and the small lakes that formed along its floor all contained a strong natron solution. When the flood receded and the lakes dried up, the natron crystallized and remained as an encrustation on the valley floor, where it could easily be scooped out.

The evidence for the use of natron in the Old Kingdom, though scanty, seems conclusive. Analysis of canopic jars of Queen Hetep-heres, the mother of King Cheops, for example, shows that the internal organs had been soaked in a solution of 3 per cent natron during mummification.

Herodotus mentions that the mummification process took over seventy days to complete. But from the Old Kingdom comes a unique text that states that the body of Queen Meres-ankh III was delivered to the House of Mummification in "year 1, first month of the third season, day 21," and was carried to her tomb on "year 2, second month of the second season, day 18," 272 days later. While these 272 days must include time for transporting the body and rituals involved with the dead as well as the mummification process itself, it is a surprisingly long time, far longer than what was usual in the New Kingdom. Zaki Iskander, presently the director-general of the Egyptian Antiquities Department, believes that in the earlier periods a solution of natron was probably used, rather than natron in solid form. Experiments he and others have conducted on chickens and pigeons show that the dehydration process takes longer when using a solution than when using solid natron.[3]

Nothing more clearly testifies to the inadequacy of these Old Kingdom techniques of mummification than the fact that so few mummies of that period are still in existence. Only about seven, in fact, can definitely be assigned an Old Kingdom date, and of these only five have been found to be relatively intact.

In 1968 the Michigan Expedition was asked by the Egyptian Antiquities Department to x-ray one of these Old Kingdom mummies, discovered only two years before at Saqqara. It is that of an official of the Fifth Dynasty named Nefer, whose tomb at Saqqara had been covered by later construction and had thereby been spared the destruction most other tombs in this necropolis had suffered.

Nefer's mummy shows clearly the techniques of the Old Kingdom embalmers. The strips of bandages in which the mummy was wrapped were first soaked in an adhesive material and were then carefully molded to reproduce the contours of the body; the genitalia were particularly well modeled. Eyes, eyebrows, and mustache were carefully drawn in ink on the molded linen. The dehydration process, which usually produced a gaunt, emaciated figure, did not have any great effect on this body, which looks more like a man asleep than a mummy. His face is full; his arms and legs still heavy and muscular. He must have looked perfectly healthy when he died in middle age. His teeth too show none of the heavy wear or abscesses found in mummies of later periods. The body, unwrapped and covered only with a piece of linen, still lies in his beautiful tomb at Saqqara.

4.

The developments of the Old Kingdom in architecture, literature, science, technology, religion, and mummification were made possible by the strong central government, which controlled the Nile from the Mediterranean to Aswan. This central authority, a centripetal force that bound together the energies of Egypt's disparate groups, for some reason collapsed about 2200 B.C., and the centrifugal forces of local independence and individualism won out. Arts, crafts, sciences, and technology, dependent upon the affluence only a unified country could provide, entered a period of provincialism and decline. This, the First Intermediate Period, lasted for over a century; if mummification was practiced during that period, no evidence of it has survived.

Not until the Eleventh Dynasty, about 2100 B.C., did a central government again begin to exert the control necessary to reunite Egypt, and not until about three or four generations later did this control become firm. This was the Middle Kingdom, from which the next evidence of mummification has come.

Though there are not a large number of mummies, all of those known show evidence of considerable advancement in the embalming technique. Dry natron, rather than natron in solution, was used. This insured a faster, more thorough dehydration of the body, an important factor in its preservation. Since this more rapid dehydration resulted in less deformation of the physical features of the body, the molding of the body parts in linen was abandoned.

Perhaps the most important advance was the development of the second technique of embalming described by Herodotus. Instead of making an incision in the abdomen to remove the internal organs, a strong solution of an oleo-resin, not unlike turpentine, was injected into the body through the rectum and was left to soak for several days. When it was removed, it brought with it the dissolved organs—a grotesque but effective method, which greatly enhanced the chances of preservation.

This new technique was not used on all mummies, for several of those examined show that abdominal incision was still practiced. In these cases the heart was left in the body. In both methods the brain was left untouched. One such mummy which has survived in good condition is that of the Lady Imenit (believed to be of the Eleventh Dynasty) which was x-rayed by the portable Ytterbium 169 Isotope unit inside her sarcophagus in the Egyptian Museum. Of special interest was the large assortment of beads made of silver, stone, and faience which lay beside the body.

5.

During the later years of the Middle Kingdom a new force was entering Egypt. People called the Hyksos were entering the Nile Valley, perhaps from Western Asia, and establishing permanent settlements in the Delta. Foreigners had come to Egypt many times before, but never in such large numbers. Perhaps through fighting, but more likely because of the weak hold the last Middle

Kingdom kings retained over the valley, Egypt collapsed under their impact. During the next three centuries, the Second Intermediate Period, foreigners were in effective control of the land. About 1600 B.C. the Egyptians regained control of their land, and with this return to power came a strong desire to return to the traditions of earlier periods.

One of the first practices to be revived during the New Kingdom was mummification. By the Eighteenth Dynasty, only a few years after the expulsion of the Hyksos, it had achieved the high degree of perfection now associated with Egyptian treatment of the dead, the meticulous and successful technique Herodotus described as being the most elaborate and expensive.

Several changes in mummification technique occurred during this period. The brain was now extracted, through the nose; the abdomen was again opened to remove the internal organs; and the abdominal cavity was packed with linen soaked in resin to present a lifelike form. The resin added to the body was heated before application to insure that it completely coated the internal cavity, thus killing any bacteria and forming an airtight seal to preserve the soft tissues.

Iskander has made an intensive study of the techniques of mummification used during the New Kingdom and has been able to reconstruct in detail the thirteen steps required.[4] These are summarized in the following paragraphs.

1. Shortly after death—exactly how long after is not known—the body was carried to the "Per-nefer," the House of Mummification, or to the "Wabet," the House of Purification. The clothing was removed, and the body was placed on a large wooden board.

2. The brain was extracted through the nostrils. A

small chisel pierced the bones of the nose, a hooked wire was passed through, and the cerebral matter was removed. The brain could also be removed through a hole made in the skull, but this was an extremely rare variation. In no case was the brain preserved with the other organs, probably because the Egyptians did not assign to the brain any special or important functions.

3. An incision was made in the abdomen, and all the contents, save the kidneys, were removed. Most scholars have generally argued that this removal of the internal organs was done simply to enhance the likelihood that the body would be preserved. But there is evidence that the reasons were also religious, as Porphyry, a Greek scholar of the third century A.D., suggested:

> There is one point which must not be passed over, namely, that when they embalm the dead of the wealthy class, among other observances paid to the corpse, they privately remove the intestines and place them in a chest, which they make fast and present before the sun, while one of those occupied in embalming the body recites a prayer. And this prayer, which Ekphantos translated from his native language, is to the following effect: "O Lord Sun and all you gods who give life to men, receive me favourably and commit me to abide with the everlasting gods. For as long as I continued in that life, I have steadfastly reverenced the gods whom my parents instructed me to worship, and I have ever honoured those who brought my body into the world, while, as concerns my fellow men, I have done no murder, nor betrayed a trust, nor committed any other deadly sin. But if during my life, I have sinned in eating or drinking what was unlawful, the

fault was not mine, but of this [showing the chest in which was the stomach].''[5]

After the abdomen was cleansed, the diaphragm was cut and all the contents of the thorax (chest cavity) except the heart were removed. To the Egyptians, the heart, and not the brain, was the seat of mind and emotion, the organ that recorded for the gods all the good and evil deeds one did during life. In religious scenes, the heart of the deceased was shown being weighed against the symbol of truth to determine whether the deceased was worthy of heaven or not. The heart, therefore, had to be kept with the body for this ceremony, described in the following chapter of the Book of the Dead, a collection of formulas, prayers, and hymns designed to facilitate travel in the afterworld:

> My heart of my mother, my heart of my mother, my heart of my being, stand not up against me at my testifying, tender no evidence against me at my judgement. Contradict me not before the judges. Make not thy tilting down for me in the presence of the guardian of the Balances. Thou art my *ka* dwelling in my body and united with it and making strong members. Come forth thou to the paradise, transport us thereto. Do not stink my name in front of the Divine Lords who make the people. Be there standing up. Be fair for us, make fair hearing at the weighing of words. Speak not lies against me in front of the Great Gods. Surely you will be lifted up living.[6]

4. After the internal organs had been removed, the thorax and abdomen were washed with palm wine and spices.

5. The viscera were separately washed and placed in a container of natron for forty days. After being sprinkled with perfume and treated with hot resin, they were wrapped in packages and placed in four canopic jars. Each jar had the head of a deity carved on the lid. After the Eighteenth Dynasty the heads were those of the Four Sons of Horus: Imsety (human-headed) guarded the liver; Hapi (ape-headed), the lungs; Dua-mutef (jackal-headed), the stomach; and Qebeh-senwef (hawk-headed), the intestines. In the Twenty-first Dynasty, instead of using canopic jars, the individually wrapped and treated organs were returned to the body, each accompanied by a wax figure of one of the Four Sons. Later, in the Twenty-sixth Dynasty, the packets were simply placed between the legs of the deceased.

6. To speed the dehydration process and prevent any disfigurement of the body, the abdominal and thoracic cavities were packed with temporary stuffing material. Sand, straw, resin, rags, dried vegetable fibers—one gets the impression that anything handy was used—were tightly packed into the cavity.

7. The seventy days of which Herodotus spoke probably represented the total time required for the entire mummification process. Almost half that time was required for dehydration, since any remaining fluids could destroy the body. This was accomplished by placing the body on a sloping board and covering it with heaps of dried natron. The time required for this operation has been the subject of dispute; the "forty days" mentioned in the Bible (Genesis 50:2–3) perhaps alludes to this:

> And Joseph commanded his servants the physicians to embalm his father: and the physicians embalmed Israel.

And forty days were fulfilled for him: for so are fulfilled the days of those which are embalmed: and the Egyptians mourned for him threescore and ten days.

Even today in Egyptian villages a ceremony for the dead is conducted forty days after death, perhaps a survival of this early tradition.

8. After the dehydration process was completed the body was removed from the natron. The temporary stuffing was taken out and, having come into contact with the dead man, was not discarded but set aside. The body was washed with water and palm wine and carefully dried.

9. Resin or resin-soaked linen was then placed in the cranial cavity, and sawdust, myrrh, occasionally onions— all carefully wrapped separately in small linen bags— were stuffed into the abdomen. During the Twenty-first Dynasty the wax figures of the Four Sons of Horus were added at this point. The abdominal incision was now sewn up, often rather crudely, and in some cases a small plate of gold or a beeswax seal was placed over it.

10. The body was rubbed with a mixture of cedar oil, cumin, wax, natron, gum, and possibly milk and wine, then dusted with spices.

11. To restore a lifelike appearance to the face, the cheeks were padded with linen and the nose was plugged. Small pads of linen were placed in the sockets, and the eyelids were closed.

12. To strengthen the skin and to prevent moisture from entering the pores, a thick coating of molten resin was applied to the entire body.

13. Occasionally the eyebrows might be painted on or jewelry used to decorate the body. Bandaging usually

began by separately wrapping each finger and toe, then each limb, and finally the body as a whole. Everything that had touched the mummy during these thirteen steps, including the stuffing materials, was now carefully gathered together, packed into sixty-seven large pots, and buried near the tomb of the deceased. This was necessary, for it was thought that the possession of so much as a hair of the deceased's head by an enemy would provide a means of bewitching him.

Placed in his coffin, accompanied by priests and mourners and members of his family, the deceased was carried in procession to the river and across to his tomb on the West Bank. Ceremonies were performed to restore his ability to see, hear, speak, move, and eat, so that he might enjoy in the afterlife all that he had enjoyed in this one. At the close of the ceremonies the priest recited these words: "You live again, you revive always, you have become young again, you are young again, and forever."[7]

Did such ceremonies work? The Egyptians believed they did, and the belief in the magical properties of mummies has persisted through the ages. Less than four hundred years ago, powdered mummy—ancient human flesh, finely ground—was prescribed by physicians as a treatment for epilepsy, heart murmurs, nausea, poisoning, paralysis, tuberculosis, cuts, bruises—in short, almost every known ailment. Genuine ancient Egyptian mummies, rather than the naturally desiccated bodies one finds in any desert country, were especially favored by physicians, and by the late 1500s an extensive trade had developed to locate and ship such mummies to druggists throughout Europe. As the demand for mummies increased, enterprising merchants "manufactured" artificial mummies, exhuming bodies from local cemeteries and drying the cadavers to produce a substance that at least looked like the real article. Some physicians of the sixteenth century, such as Ambroise Paré, criticized the use of mummy, claiming that it caused "many troublesome symptoms, as paine of the heart or stomake, vomitting, and stinke of the mouth."[8] But its use has continued. Even today there is a regular, though admittedly not very heavy, demand at a New York pharmacy catering to witches for genuine powdered Egyptian mummy. The cost is forty dollars an ounce.

THREE ✝ THE MUMMY DEFILED
—Tombs and Tomb Robbers

The most interesting and important of the New Kingdom mummies are those of the pharaohs. Thirty-three royal mummies are known from this period, and the story of how this remarkable collection reached the Egyptian Museum demonstrates a fatal flaw in the Egyptians' plan of immortality: human greed was not taken into account.

1.

The village of Sheikh Abd el-Qurneh lies on the slopes of the ancient Theban necropolis, a two-cent ferry ride across the Nile and a long, invariably overpriced trip by donkey west of modern Luxor. The banks of the Nile are fertile, its broad valley green and prosperous, but these pleasant features are left behind as one continues west toward the village, which lies several hundred yards beyond the cultivation, on the edge of the Great Western

Desert. The macadam road through the fields does not approach the village, and the last part of the journey is made on foot over dust-covered mounds of sand and rock, so heated by the sun that even the heavy soles of boots offer little protection.

The first signs that the village lies close by are its sounds: barking dogs, young goats crying for their mothers, children at play in the narrow streets. The brilliant sunlight erases details of the landscape, makes it appear two-dimensional. One is practically in the village before it is seen: drab, sand-colored walls of sun-dried brick, difficult to distinguish from the hillside itself, built close together whenever possible to provide small patches of welcome shade in the late afternoon. Among the walls and the rocky slopes, doorways carved into the bedrock itself lead to subterranean shelters for the villagers and their animals. Giovanni Belzoni, an Italian adventurer who explored—and exploited—Egyptian antiquities, visited Qurneh in 1820; he described the houses thus:

> The people . . . live in the entrance of such caves as have already been opened, and, by making partitions with earthen walls, they form habitations for themselves, as well as for their cows, camels, buffaloes, sheep, goats, dogs, etc. . . . Their dwelling is generally in the passage between the first and second entrance into a tomb. The walls and the roof are as black as any chimney. The inner door is closed up with mud, except a small aperture sufficient for a man to crawl through. Within this place the sheep are kept at night, and occasionally accompany their masters in their vocal concert.[1]

From the village the cultivated fields seem unreal through the waves of hot, dust-laden air. Only a mile away the Qurnawis (so men from Qurneh are called) could find many sites more hospitable for a village, sites with fresh water and trees and cool, fertile fields. But for them the location of their village is ideal. They earn their living here, on these hot, desolate slopes, not in the nearby fields.

Close by Qurneh lie the tombs in which the ancient Egyptian rulers and noblemen were buried with all the grave goods their religion decreed essential for the afterlife. Beneath the village's mud foundations lie the Tombs of the Nobles: hundreds of rock-cut chambers carved to protect the remains of those who administered Egypt over three thousand years ago. The Valley of the Kings and the Valley of the Queens are half an hour's walk farther west. Deep in rugged limestone cliffs, over forty pharaohs were buried, surrounded by the splendor appropriate to their rank. The only royal tomb archaeologists have found intact is that of Tutankhamon, who was, in fact, a minor king. It consists of four small chambers, and their riches must only hint at the care and expense that must have been lavished on the burials of more powerful rulers.

For many years the Qurnawis made a good living from plundering these tombs: robbing them of their amulets and scarabs, precious jewelry and papyri, and selling their finds to the antiquities dealers across the river in Luxor. Careful to sell only a few objects at a time, regular in giving baksheesh (bribes) to the police, they rarely encountered trouble. However much they managed to take from the tombs, there seemed no end to the treasure.

Yet the Qurnawis were certainly not the first to engage

in this traffic. Tomb robbing had been a major—and profitable—activity at Thebes even in ancient times.

For the last three thousand years a war of wits has been waged by those sworn to protect the tombs of Egypt's ancient rulers and those set on plundering their treasure. In ancient times that protection was the duty of the priests, who depended upon vigilance, secrecy, and the promised wrath of the gods to thwart the plunderers. In more recent times the Egyptian Antiquities Service, with its own local site guards, has been assigned this responsibility and has threatened prompt and heavy penalties for theft. But no matter how zealously the priests and the guards have carried out their duty, the thieves have continued stealing and have rarely been caught. They have ignored the threat of imprisonment and painful interrogation in modern times just as they ignored such promises of wrath as those inscribed on be-half of Amenhotep, son of Hapu, nearly four thousand years ago. That inscription reads in part: "[Trespassers in my tomb] shall not receive the honours which are given virtuous men; they shall have no son to succeed them; their wives shall be raped before their eyes. . . ."[2]

Dealers in antiquities had a ready market for whatever objects the Qurnawis brought them. From the 1860s on, European tourists were visiting Luxor in increasing numbers, to take advantage of its many historic sites and the winter sun. For the men of Qurneh these years were consistently profitable. For one villager in particular, a man named Ahmed Abd el-Rassoul, the year 1871 and the decade that followed were to be years of unparalleled success.

The details are not clear for there is much conflicting testimony, but the story is told that one afternoon, while tending his herd of goats in the necropolis, Ahmed went looking for a kid that had become separated from its mother. The slopes of the necropolis are treacherous for an unwary animal, pocketed with deep shafts dug by the ancient Egyptians as entrances to tombs that often were abandoned and never used. In one of these, a shaft about six feet wide and forty feet deep, he spied the kid. As he climbed down to retrieve it, fragments of ancient objects in the sand at the bottom piqued his curiosity and he began scraping at the compact debris. On the west side of the shaft, his fingers touched the outline of an opening hidden by the sand, which proved to be a doorway sealed with stones and plaster. He made a small hole through the sealed threshold; peering through, he could see statuettes, amulets, and papyri—more antiquities than he had ever seen before—and mummies deeply stacked in piles that extended far beyond the thin beam of light penetrating the interior.

Excited by the importance of the discovery, Ahmed enlisted the aid of his brother Mohammed, and together with his son they soon began removing the objects from the chamber. Crossing the Nile at regular intervals in later months, their plunder carefully concealed in their clothing or hidden in baskets of vegetables, they sold the pieces, a few at a time, to the Luxor antiquities dealers. During the next ten years they made only infrequent trips to the cache for more. Too many antiquities at one time might lower the prices and invite suspicion.

The man who purchased a number of these pieces, and who soon became the only one to whom the two brothers sold, was an unusual character named Mustapha Agha Ayat. A Turk settled in Luxor, Ayat had managed to have himself appointed consular agent for Great Britain, Belgium, and Russia, and represented the interests of their nationals traveling in Upper Egypt. His post gave him the valuable benefit of diplomatic immunity, and he used it to the fullest, buying and shipping antiquities through Egyptian Customs to his clientele abroad.

Neither Ayat nor the Abd el-Rassoul brothers noticed, however, that most of the pieces they were selling from the cache were of a type seen rarely, if at all, on the marketplace: royal funerary papyri, shawabtis (figures, whose purpose was to act on behalf of the deceased for many tasks in the afterworld), scarabs, canopic jars with the names of kings of the Twentieth Dynasty—pieces whose existence had been suspected but which had not yet been found. Eventually reports of their sale filtered in to the Antiquities Service.

News of their appearance made it clear to the director, Gaston Maspero, that an important discovery had been made at Thebes and was systematically being plundered. In 1881 he telegraphed the police in Luxor to keep careful watch on anyone who might be involved in such illicit operations. He sent one of his staff to Luxor, where the man pretended to be a tourist interested in acquiring antiquities and not concerned about the usual formalities. Both avenues of investigation soon pointed clearly to Mustapha Ayat and the Abd el-Rassoul brothers. Ayat, of course, could not be prosecuted because of his diplomatic immunity, but the brothers could, and on April 4, 1881, their arrest was ordered. Two days later, after their homes had been searched—unsuccessfully, of course, for they were not so foolish as to store antiquities there—they were sent in chains to the town of Qeneh, the residence of the police administrator, about thirty miles from Luxor, for interrogation.

One historian has described the examination that followed as a theatrical tragicomedy. It is an appropriate comparison. Maspero had ordered Daud Pasha, the mayor of Qeneh, to preside at the hearing. Because of a severe skin ailment, the mayor sat through the trial submerged to his neck in a jar of water. The interrogation itself followed procedures little changed since ancient times. Torture was used to elicit confessions, and several years later Ahmed was still showing the scars left from beatings and ropes and heated iron pots that had been placed over his head.

Yet, as one might have expected, the trial produced no results, and the brothers were released in the custody of their family. A large contingent of fellow Qurnawis had come to Qeneh for the hearing, and an impressive array of character witnesses had come forth to attest to the honesty of the Abd el-Rassoul family, solemnly swearing that they, of all their people, and Ahmed especially, were highly respected and definitely not likely to defile an ancient tomb.

It was only a short time after they had returned to Qurneh, however, that an argument broke out between the two brothers. Ahmed insisted that the suffering he had endured during the trial entitled him to half the proceeds of the robberies. Mohammed and the other family members now involved in the scheme insisted upon the one-fifth shares originally agreed on.

Ahmed's demands were vocal, and the fighting between him and Mohammed soon became common knowledge to the Qurnawis and, a short time later, to the Antiquities Service. Mohammed, perhaps knowing how rumors of their arguments had spread, decided that there was nothing to do but try to save himself and confess. Early in July he traveled secretly to Qeneh and told the entire story of the robberies to Daud Pasha. Promised immunity from punishment, he dictated the details of the discovery and the theft, pointing to his brother as the leader of the plan.

On July 6, 1881, accompanied by Emil Brugsch, a German Egyptologist on the staff of the Antiquities Service, and Brugsch's assistant, Mohammed returned to Qurneh to show the authorities where the cache lay. They climbed the steep hillside to the well-hidden shaft. Brugsch had come armed, and he and his assistant were justifiably nervous as they stood at the top of the forty-foot-deep excavation. He remembered the trial, and he knew that Ahmed was well liked in his village and that Mohammed's confession might bring reprisals.

Wasting no time, Brugsch fixed a rope around his waist and let himself be lowered down the shaft. He waited only a moment when his feet touched the sand, to let his eyes adjust to the dim light, before stepping over the threshold. He lit a candle, and its thin rays penetrated the dark chamber.

Movement in the chamber was difficult. The ceiling was only four and one-half feet high, and wherever Brugsch looked the floor was covered with bronze bowls and vessels, wooden shrines and exquisitely carved statuettes, canopic jars whose lids were sculpted with the animal heads of deities. He was no more than two feet inside the passage when the candle shone upon a painted coffin bearing the name Neskhonsu, wife of the High Priest of the Twentieth Dynasty, and a few feet farther on he found those of Queen Henttowy and King Seti I. A funerary tent in which mortuary services had been conducted lay cast aside in a corner. Lifting it from the dust, he could read the name of Queen Esemkhebe. As he moved down the passageway, more and more coffins appeared, bearing the names of such famous rulers as Amenhotep I, Thutmosis II, Ahmose, and Ramesses II.

The chamber, three meters wide and nearly two hundred meters long, was filled with the bodies and the treasures of more kings than any modern man had ever seen. Little wonder that Brugsch was later to say that it all seemed like a dream, something impossible to believe was real. Maspero agreed: "Like him, I ask myself if I am not dreaming when I see and touch the bodies of so many rulers of whom we thought we always would know only the name."[3]

The magnitude of the Deir el-Bahri discovery and the possibility of further thefts demanded prompt action, and Brugsch wasted no time telegraphing the Antiquities Service and arranging for the removal of this find to the Egyptian Museum. That same day he hired three hundred workmen, and he and his assistants supervised the delicate task of raising the sarcophagi and their contents from the chamber, carrying them across the desert and the fields, and loading them on the government boat *el-Menshieh*. Forty-eight hours later the first load headed northward toward Cairo.

News of the move spread rapidly, and as the boat sailed past small villages, hundreds of fellahin (peasants) lined the river's edge to pay tribute to their former kings. Women wailed and tore their hair; men solemnly fired their shotguns into the air. It was a traditional funeral. These kings who had lain at Thebes for three thousand years were now leaving forever.

Mohammed Abd el-Rassoul was rewarded for his confession with a gift of five hundred pounds sterling and appointed as chief of the Antiquities Service guards in the necropolis. Ahmed presumably went back to the quiet life of the shepherd—but only for a time.

A hundred years later, the antiquities market was still receiving part of its merchandise from the men at Sheikh Abd el-Qurneh, and over the years the attempts of the government to move them, to settle them in an agricultural life in a fine new village, have failed.

⬧ 2.

Several thousand years before Abd el-Rassoul began plundering antiquities, the violation of tombs at Thebes was a thriving business. The Royal Architect Ineny, who supervised construction of the tombs of the pharaohs Amenhotep I and Thutmosis I about 1500 B.C., wrote: "I supervised the carving of the tomb of His Majesty in a solitary place, none seeing, none hearing."[4] But even as those words were being carved, he almost certainly was aware that thieves did know of the tombs and were anxiously awaiting the day they could safely be plundered. The lure of the treasures such burials contained was far stronger than any deterrent that might be encountered.

There is good evidence to indicate that very often the men supposedly guarding the tombs—the necropolis police and the priests—were in fact involved in these robberies. Consequently official action was rarely taken against the plunderers since only rarely were the robberies reported. When, in the latter part of the New Kingdom, during the reigns of the Ramesside kings between 1200 and 1085 B.C., the tomb robbing became outrageously obvious, some action had to be taken. The details have come down almost complete, in one of the most fascinating series of papyri known from ancient Egypt.[5]

In August, 1126 B.C., upset by persistent rumors of thefts in the Great Necropolis, the mayor of Eastern

Thebes, a man named Pa-ser, began an investigation to determine which of the royal tombs had been violated. Such a decision should really have been made by Pa-wero, the mayor of Western Thebes, since the necropolis lay on the West Bank of the Nile and was under his jurisdiction, but Pa-ser had reason to suspect that Pa-wero was himself involved in the plundering. Furthermore, the two mayors seem to have been bitter rivals, and Pa-ser undoubtedly saw in this an opportunity to discredit Pa-wero as well as to end the thefts.

According to a document found at Thebes in the 1850s and known today as Papyrus Amherst, Pa-ser managed to locate several suspects. With a scribe from his office recording the interrogation, confessions were extracted from several of the accused men. One of them, whose name unfortunately is lost, told this story.

> . . . Now in year 13 of the Pharaoh my Lord, four years ago, I agreed with the carpenter Seteknakht [to rob the tombs of the Necropolis. We searched] and we found the tomb of [the King] and of the Royal Wife, Neb-khaas. It was protected and sealed with plaster, but we forced it open. We opened their coffins and the cloth in which they were wrapped and found the noble mummy of the King, equipped like a warrior. There were many sacred eye amulets and ornaments of gold at his neck, and a mask of gold upon him. The noble mummy of the King was covered completely with gold and silver, inside and out, and with inlays of all sorts of precious stones. We took the gold which we found on this noble mummy of this god, and his eye amulets, and the ornaments which were at his neck and on the wrappings in which he lay. We found the Royal Wife

similarly adorned and we took all that we found on her, too. We set fire to the wrappings. We stole their equipment which we found on them, objects of gold, silver and bronze, and divided them among ourselves. We divided the gold which we found on these two gods and on their mummies into eight parts. . . . Then we crossed over to Thebes. A few days later the district superintendents heard of our stealing in the West and they seized me and imprisoned me in the office of the Mayor of Thebes.[6]

Armed with clear confessions, Pa-ser went the next day to the vizier, Kha-em-wese, and requested that an examination of the royal tombs be made to determine which had been violated. Papyrus Abbot, a summary of that investigation made for the temple archives, describes the event.

Year 16, third month of the season of Inundation, day 18, under the Majesty of the King of Upper and Lower Egypt, the Lord of the Two Lands, Nefer-kare-Setepenre (life, prosperity and health!), the Son of Re, the Lord of Diadems, Ramesses Mery-Amon, the Beloved of Amon-Re, the King of the Gods and of Re, Horus of the Horizon, granted life forever unto eternity.

On this day the Inspector of the Great and Splendid Necropolis, the Scribe of the Vizier, and the Overseer of the Palace Treasury were sent by the Vizier Kha-em-wese [and others who are listed] to examine the tombs of former kings and the graves and resting-places of the favored ones which lie on the west of the City, and to discover the thieves on the west of the City whom the Prince Pa-wero, Chief of the Desert Police of the Necropolis, had reported to the Vizier.

The pyramids, tombs and graves examined this day by the Inspectors:

The eternal tomb of King Djeserkare, Son of Re, Amenhotep, which measures 120 cubits in depth [about 560 feet] from its superstructure, the high point north of the house of Amenhotep of the Orchard. The Prince of Thebes, Pa-ser, had reported to the Overseer of Thebes, and the Vizier Kha-em-wese, stating that the thieves had violated it. Examined this day by the Inspectors, it was found unharmed.[7]

Pa-wero, it seems, had friends in high places, for the tour of inspection is described as being held at his request. Little wonder that the inspectors carefully chose the tombs they would examine, missing no opportunity to show Pa-ser in the wrong. There were, however, violations in one royal tomb and several private tombs that could not be ignored.

The pyramid-tomb of King Sekhcmre-Shedtawy, Son of Re, Sobek-em-saf: the thieves had broken into it by tunneling through the lower chamber of its pyramid from the outer hall of the tomb of the Overseer of the Granary of King Menkheperre, Nebamon. The burial chamber of the King was found empty of its Lord, as was the burial chamber of the Great Royal Wife, Neb-khaas, his Consort. The thieves had laid their hands upon them. The Vizier, the Nobles and the Butlers investigated it, and the manner in which the thieves had laid their hands upon the King and his Consort was determined. . . .

The graves and tombs in which the favored ones of former times and the female citizens and the people of the land rest, on the west of the City: it was found that the thieves had violated them all, dragging their owners from their coffins and their wrappings, throwing them onto the desert, and stealing the funerary furniture which they had been given, together with the gold and silver and the equipment which were in their wrappings.[8]

In other circumstances, such evidence would have served to bring Pa-wero to trial for dereliction of duty at the very least, but because of his tight control of the situation he emerged from the investigation victorious. He crowed that far fewer tombs had been violated than Pa-ser had claimed, and that his administration and his supervision of the necropolis police were thereby vindicated.

Pa-ser continued to seek evidence proving his initial charges (which were true, of course) but met with little success. Thieves from whom he would elicit confessions later maintained their innocence before the vizier and were freed. Tombs that he claimed had been plundered would be examined and found to be shafts that had never been used. Pa-ser seems not to have realized how completely the necropolis was in the hands of Pa-wero and how slim were his chances of convincing an already biased administration of wrongdoing.

A few months after his series of defeats before the vizier's court, Pa-ser was sitting at home when a group of Pa-wero's supporters crossed the Nile and spent the evening, probably drunk, carousing at his door, taunting him because of his unsuccessful attempt to oust their master. Angrily Pa-ser stalked off to the Temple of Ptah at Karnak and spent some time talking to the king's butler, Nesuamon, whom he met there. The hecklers followed from his home and soon appeared at the temple, continuing their teasing.

Pa-ser lost his temper. He reiterated all his old charges against Pa-wero and added several new ones, listing other tombs he knew to have been plundered. This time, he said, he would write the story of the thefts directly to the pharaoh rather than to the vizier. This was a mistake. It was contrary to the rules of bureaucratic etiquette and obviously implied that the vizier himself was a party to the robberies.

Nesuamon seems to have been anxious to ingratiate himself with the vizier, Kha-em-wese, for the next document is a letter to him:

> I heard the words which the Prince of Thebes spoke to the people of the Great and Noble Necropolis, and I [herewith] report them to my Lord. For it would be a sin if one in my position heard [such] a thing and concealed it.[9]

The result was predictable. Kha-em-wese convened another court and, with obvious exasperation, argued that all of Pa-ser's many claims had been examined, all his witnesses questioned, all the tombs inspected, and that the charges were completely without foundation. Pa-ser, he implied, should quit his malicious trouble-making and go back to more constructive work. It was Pa-ser's worst defeat. The tomb robbing continued unabated.

During the next two years Pa-ser continued to submit charges against the thieves to the vizier, and once, about twelve months after his embarrassing hearing before Kha-em-wese, actually got the vizier to visit another tomb. This time it was one that had been violated and could not be ignored. Perhaps it was in part because of this discovery, which this time Kha-em-wese was forced to admit, that the vizier disappears from the records.

A new vizier, Nebmare-nakht, was appointed. He had served for about eighteen months when a list of necropolis thieves was placed before him and the pharaoh. The men on the list were apprehended—there were forty-five in all—and full-scale trials were held. After nearly four years of work, Pa-ser's charges and the other evidence of theft were being honestly examined.

Parts of the transcripts of those trials have been preserved. Ironically, the papyri in which the trials were recorded made their way to various museums after being sold on the Luxor antiquities market by thieves who had stolen them from Theban tombs. One trial was held "in the city of Thebes, by order of the vizier, in the nineteenth year of the Pharaoh Ramesses XI [1095 B.C.]."

> . . . fourth month of summer, day five. An examination was made on this day of the great enemies, the thieves who had trespassed in the Great Tombs. . . .
>
> *Examination.* The Inspector Pa-yer-soker of the Temple of Amon was brought. He was given the oath to the Ruler, saying, "If I lie may I be mutilated and placed on the stake."
>
> They say to him: "What is the story of your going to rob the Great Tombs? What have you to say?"
>
> He said: "Far be it from me [to rob a tomb], far be it from me."
>
> He was beaten with a stick [until] he said: "Stop! I will confess!" But he did not. . . .

Examination. The Incense-Roaster of the Temple of Amon, Shedsu-khonsu, was brought.

He was asked: "Tell me some of the men who were with you in the Tombs."

He said: "I was asleep in my house [when] Amon-khau and the foreigner Userhet-nakht and the trumpeter Per-pet-khau and the Incense-Roaster Nes-amon came. [It was] night. They said to me, 'Come out. We are going to take plunder for bread to eat.' They took me with them. We opened the tomb and brought away a shroud of gold and silver. We broke it up, put it into a basket, brought it down and divided it up into six parts. We gave two parts to Amon-khau, for he said it was he who had pointed out [the tomb] to us. . . ."

Examination. The Trumpeter of the Temple of Amon, Amon-khau, was brought.

The Vizier asked him: "What is the story of your going with the Incense-Roaster Shedsu-khonsu when you attacked this Great Tomb and took from it the silver after the thieves had been there?"

He said: "Far be it from me. Per-pet-khau, the trumpeter, is an enemy of mine. I quarreled with him and I told him, 'You will be put to death for this theft which you have committed in the Necropolis.' He said to me, 'If I go [to my death], I will take you with me.' So he said to me."

He was examined with the stick on his feet and his hands [until] he said, "I saw no one at all. If I had seen, I would tell." He was then examined with the birch and the screw.*

---

*Physical measures were customarily used to obtain confessions. The "stick" and the "birch" were used to thrash or beat the prisoner, and the "screw" was applied to the extremities, usually the fingers. Similar methods were employed until quite recently.

He said: "I saw nothing at all. If I had seen, I would tell. . . ."

Examination. The Incense-Roaster of the Temple of Amon, Nes-amon, called Tjebay, was brought. He was given the oath to the Ruler, saying: "If I lie may I be mutilated and sent to Nubia."

They said to him: "Tell [us] the story of going with your cohorts to attack the Great Tombs. . . ."

He said: "We went to a tomb and brought some vessels of silver from it, and we divided them among the five of us." He was examined with the stick. He said: "I saw nothing else. I have told what I saw." Again he was examined with the stick [until] he said: "Stop! I will tell."

The Vizier asked him: "What were the vessels which you brought away?"

"Some vases of silver and furniture parts of gold. . . ." He was [then] examined with the stick and he said: "We brought away [only] the treasure I have specifically mentioned."

The Vizier [then] said to him: "Tell me the men who were with you."

He said: "There was the merchant Pa-nefery of Merwer, together with the men whom the other thieves have [already] listed." He was again examined with the stick and he said: "Stop! I will tell. [We] took the silver shroud from the tomb. We broke it up, put it in a basket, and divided it among the five of us."

The Scribe of the Necropolis, Thutmose, said: "He brought away the vases of silver and the furniture from one tomb, but the tomb from which he took the shroud is another. [This makes] two tombs [which he robbed]."

He was examined with the stick [until] he said: "Stop! I will tell. This silver is [all] that we brought out. I saw nothing else." He was examined with the birch and the screw, and he said: "Stop! . . . This is the complete story of my deeds. . . ."

Nesy-amenope, the Scribe of the Necropolis, said to him: "Then the tomb from which you said the vases of silver were taken is [yet] another tomb. That makes two [tombs] besides the main treasure."

He said: "That is false. The vases belong to the main treasure I have already told you about. We opened one tomb and only one."

He was examined again with the stick and the birch and the screw [but] he would not confess anything beyond what he had [already] said.[10]

The papyri do not mention the final outcome of these trials, but it seems fair to assume that those who were found guilty were dealt with severely. However, any decline in the frequency of tomb robberies was probably short-lived.

Such trials were conducted on several occasions during the next few decades, and at least one result was a much greater concern by the priests for the safeguarding of the royal mummies in their charge. On several of the mummies taken from the cache at Thebes to Cairo in 1881 were inscriptions, written in ink on the wrappings, that told how the priests had taken the pharaoh's body from his tomb when they found it plundered and had hidden it elsewhere. The cache discovered by Ahmed Abd el-Rassoul, in fact, was the result of such an attempt to safeguard these remains. It was only luck that had prevented that cache from being discovered three millennia earlier.

On the coffin of Pharaoh Ramesses II, for example, an inscription tells how his body had to be moved from one hiding place to another to thwart the thieves:

> . . . day 17. The day of bringing [the mummy of] King Usermare-Setepenre [Ramesses II], the Great God, out from the tomb of King —— [Seti I] in order to bring him into the tomb of (Queen) Inhapi. That which is in good condition before me, no harm shall befall it, through my bringing them [*sic*] out from the tomb in which they rest, and they shall be taken into the tomb of (Queen) Inhapi . . . wherein King Amenhotep rests.[11]

How futile that wish! The mummy was moved at least three times before it was discovered and plundered by the Abd el-Rassoul family in A.D. 1871, and not until the 1880s did it finally come safely to rest in the Egyptian Museum.

In 1898, seventeen years after Brugsch had brought the mummies found by Abd el-Rassoul to Cairo, a cache comparable in importance was discovered at Thebes. The French Egyptologist Victor Loret, searching the Valley of the Kings, located what was obviously a royal burial carved in a small spur of the valley. On excavation, this proved to be the tomb of Amenhotep II, a king of the Eighteenth Dynasty. The innermost chamber had been reused by priests of a later period as a hiding place for thirteen mummies—among them the pharaohs Amenhotep III, Thutmosis IV, Merenptah, Siptah, Seti I, and Amenhotep II himself.

Loret decided to remove twelve of the mummies to the Egyptian Museum. Amenhotep II was left in his tomb, where he had lain for three thousand years. He was one of the very few kings ever to be found in the tomb in which he was originally buried. To protect him, he was sealed behind barred doors in the chamber.

Not long after this, the guards of the tomb were overpowered, the tomb was entered, and thieves tore open the mummy and stole the amulets and grave goods. Howard Carter (1873–1939), the British archaeologist who later was to discover the tomb of Tutankhamon, recorded the event in his journal:

The night-guards of Biban el-Moluk [the Valley of the Kings] . . . say that: —On the 24th of November [1901], slightly after sunset, whilst they were sitting down, eating their food, in the tomb No. 10, they were suddenly surprised by thirteen armed men with covered faces and that they were threatened to be shot if they moved or attempted to make an alarm. Six men remained over them whilst seven apparently went and robbed the tomb of Amenophis II [Amenhotep] and got away together with their plunder, the remaining six men then released the guards and went away by the path over the hill towards Medinet Habu. The guards rushed out after the robbers, but were shot at three times from the pathway above, and, on being frightened, returned to the tomb No. 10. A short time afterwards they came out again and inspected the tombs, finding that of Amenophis II to be forced open, the lock being broken. One of them at once went to the Inspector and reported what had happened, whilst the other two remained over the tomb; this was about the [sic] after sunset.

[An inspection of the tomb was ordered by the supervisor of the guards. The next day the police were informed and a search for the thieves begun.]

The guards having stated that they recognized three men out of the thirteen robbers—namely Abd er-Rasol [el-Rassoul] Ahmed, Adberrachman Ahmed Abd er-Rasol and Mohammed Abderrachman—of Goorneh [Qurneh]—these men were arrested by the Ombdeh [the local mayor] the same night (25th November), they being found in their houses. The above three guards were locked up also.[12]

Members of the Abd el-Rassoul family, previously encountered as the plunderers of the Deir el-Bahri cache, were plundering again. But more proof was needed before they could be charged and tried. On November 27, using those skills common to both archaeology and detective work, Carter began a minute examination of the scene of the crime and of the village.

I went over to Goorneh, Mr. Hazel and the moawen [an officer] of the police accompanying me. I had all the houses searched where I thought to find something which might throw some light upon the case. Nothing was obtained by this movement. I then went to the tomb of Amenophis II with Mr. Hazel, and found that the bandages of the royal mummy had been ripped open, but the body not broken. This had evidently been done by an expert, as the places where objects are generally found had only been touched. I carefully examined the wrappings to see if there were any signs of their having contained jewellery, but could find no traces whatsoever and concluded that no jewellery had been found or stolen. The smaller chamber, containing the three bodies, had not been touched. The boat in the antechamber had been stolen; the mummy that was upon it was lying on the floor, and had been smashed to pieces; the wire-netting enclosure that had been placed to protect it from the visitors, was bent down at one of the top corners so as to get in by and pass the boat through, a wooden stool that was in the tomb being used as an aid to climb over by. The marks of the iron gate and the lock, now in the hands of the parquet [public prosecutor], shew that it had been broken by a lever. . . .

The following day I again went to the tomb of Amenophis II with the moawen of the police, and having obtained the necessary rope, etc., we searched the well to see if possibly anything had been thrown down, but we found nothing. I then searched the whole tomb carefully for any traces of the thieves. It had been reported to me formerly by the parquet that the padlock of the tomb had been stuck together and made to look all right by means of little pieces of lead paper, which had already caused suspicion against the guards, both on the part of the parquet and myself. It being very improbable that the robbers, if they, as in the guards' statement, had rifled the tomb by force, should attempt to hide the theft by remending the lock. The result of my searches was that I found more small pieces of lead paper beneath the door and a little round piece of resin, probably from a sont-tree. This piece was the exact size of the socket for tongue in the padlock and gave me a small clue; for, on the 11th Nov., I had found that the tomb of Yi-ma-dua . . . had been broken into, the lock being forced by a lever and made to look all right by the means of resin that stuck it together, the material and method in both cases being exactly the same. . . .

I must add before going on further that I had grave suspicions against Mohammed Abd er-Rasol in the case of the Yi-ma-dua tomb, and I watched this man whenever possible, he being a well-known tomb plunderer and his house being quite near the tomb.

. . . I carefully compared the footprints in both tombs and found them to have a strong resemblance. In both cases, *the foot prints, being of bare feet, are of one person only.* Recognizing in the tomb of Amenophis II those of [several of the guards], they all wearing boots, I then took photographs, to scale as near as possible, of the foot marks of bare feet, and measured them up very carefully.

During the mean time the spoor-man [tracker] tracked foot prints from Biban el-Moluk to the village of Goorneh and to the house of Soleman and Ahmed Abd er-Rasol. These men were arrested.

I went to the parquet and informed him of these details, together with my suspicions, and requested to inspect the foot prints of Mohammed Abd er-Rasol. This I did . . . and found them to agree with my photographs and with the measurements which I had taken in the tomb of Amenophis II and Yi-ma-dua. The measurements of these contestations agreed to a millimeter.[13]

The case against the Abd el-Rassouls was strengthened the next day when it was learned that Mohammed had been seen at a blacksmith shop a few days before the robbery, carrying a bar of iron. He had told the blacksmith he wanted it as a "tomb testing rod"; it was, in fact, the lever used to pry open the tomb's lock.

The reconstructed evidence was sufficient to convict the Abd el-Rassoul brothers, twenty years after they were caught at Deir el-Bahri.

The attempts to safeguard and preserve the pharaoh and his courtiers only rarely succeeded. More often than not, they simply delayed the inevitable. There was much more truth in a song engraved on the walls of several Middle Kingdom tombs than the ancient Egyptians might have cared to admit:

> *What has been done with them? . . .*
> *What are their places [now]?*
> *Their walls have crumbled and their places*
>   *are not—*
> *As if they had never been.*
> *No one has [ever] come back from [the dead],*
> *That he might describe their condition,*
> *And relate their needs;*
> *That he might calm our hearts*
> *Until we [too] pass into that place where*
>   *they have gone. . . .*
> *[Let us] make holiday and never tire of it!*
> *[For] behold, no man can take his property*
>   *with him,*
> *No man who has gone can return again.* [14]

The royal mummies have been moved several times since their arrival in Cairo, occasionally from one museum gallery to another, once briefly to a storeroom when someone argued that the remains of Egypt's ancient kings should rest in dignity, not subject to the inquisitive eyes of tourists.

Now they are again on exhibit. Instead of in a richly gilded sarcophagus, each mummy lies in an oak coffin under a sheet of leaded glass, covered with a single piece of ancient linen. No prayer or figures of gods protect this resting place; only a lone museum guard, unsure of the names of his charges. Each day a few visitors to the museum pay the extra piasters to enter this stark room and walk among the mortal remains of the royalty that one hundred generations of priests and guards have tried to protect.

FOUR ✝ THE PHARAOH'S MUMMY
—Examination of the Imperial Dead

In 1889 Maspero conducted a brief examination of the royal mummies brought to the Egyptian Museum in Cairo, and in 1912 Smith undertook a more thorough study. Both scholars were severely limited in their research by the fact that some of the mummies could not be unwrapped, and none could be dissected. Only superficial anatomical examination was permitted, and if the mummy was well wrapped they learned nothing at all. Not until x-ray techniques were developed could the wrapping be penetrated without damaging the mummy. The Michigan Expedition was organized, as we have said, to employ these techniques in a comprehensive study. To understand the results of this work in proper historical perspective, it is necessary to return to the beginning of the New Kingdom, some thirty-six hundred years ago.

1.

It was not until 1600 B.C., during the late Seventeenth Dynasty, that there arose in Thebes a family that would prove strong enough to expel the Hyksos from Lower Egypt and maintain control of the throne of a unified country. Senakhtenre Tao, a man of common birth, and his wife Tetisheri, also born of non-royal parents, became rulers only of the land still under the control of Thebes. How they achieved their power has remained a mystery: Tao may have been related to an earlier king of the Seventeenth Dynasty, Antef V, or he may have usurped the throne. In any case it is clear that he and his wife founded the most powerful line of rulers Egypt was ever to know. Their descendants reigned for three hundred years.

Of Tao almost nothing is known; his mummy has not been found. Tetisheri, during the Eighteenth Dynasty, became the center of a popular tradition heralding her as the mother of the line of New Kingdom rulers. She outlived her husband by several years, and during the reign of her grandson a number of buildings were erected to perpetuate her memory and maintained by substantial donations.

One of the mummies from the Deir el-Bahri cache is believed to be Tetisheri. Formerly labeled an "unknown woman B," the mummy is that of an elderly woman, about five feet, two inches tall, with artificial braids intertwined with her own white hair to hide a noticeable degree of baldness. The preliminary identification was made on the basis of how she was mummified, and to confirm it the Michigan Expedition used x-rays. If she was the mother of the new line of rulers in Egypt, the features of later kings and queens might be traceable back to her.

Her head, broken from the badly damaged body, was one of the first studied. X-rays showed the same prominent dentition, the same type of malocclusion, and the same shape of the skull as the women found in the royal caches of the next four generations. The moderate wear on her teeth and even an impacted third molar, which lay at a very disfunctional angle in the jaw, were the same sort of problems found among her descendants. A comparison of this mummy, now confidently called Tetisheri, with those of her daughter Ahhotep and her granddaughter Ahmose-Nefertiry showed how well she fit this family group.

Tetisheri's role as mother of the line was strengthened because both males and females of the next several generations could trace their ancestry directly to her. This was made possible by a series of consanguineous (brother-sister) marriages. These were undoubtedly politically motivated, to insure continuity and prevent usurpation of the throne. (It is worth noting that modern studies of such marriages, especially first-cousin marriages, have shown that unless unfavorable genetic traits already are present there are no deleterious effects from such unions.)

The son of Senakhtenre Tao and Tetisheri, Seqenenre Tao, unlike his father was unable to ignore the Hyksos rulers in the north, and there is some evidence to suggest that he led a battle against the hated enemy. A text relating the legendary cause of that battle has been found. It dates from some four hundred years after his death and tells of a puzzling encounter between Seqenenre Tao and the Hyksos king Apophis.

Apophis sent a messenger to the court in Thebes protesting that the hippopotamuses in that city were so noisy that he could not sleep, and should be done away with. For a long time it was assumed by scholars that this was simply a trumped-up charge made by Apophis as a pretext for war. After all, he lived several hundred miles from the capital. But it has been pointed out that the Theban kings considered the ritual harpooning of the hippopotamus as a symbolic means of safeguarding their royal power. Further, the hippopotamus was one of the forms of the major deity of the Hyksos, Seth. Thus this complaint of Apophis could be interpreted as a challenge to the authority of the Theban throne and an insult to the pharaoh's ability to rule.

Did Seqenenre Tao retaliate and engage in war with Apophis? It cannot be certain, but it does seem likely that a small-scale battle was fought. The most compelling evidence for this is the body of Seqenenre Tao himself. His mummy and coffin were found in the Deir el-Bahri cache, where they had been placed after the reign of Ramesses IX. An examination of the body shows that the king was about thirty years old when he died and that he was killed by violent means.

Two explantions have been offered. One is that he was assassinated by members of his own court at Thebes. Among the wounds is one deep in the back of his neck, make by a dagger, and suggesting that he was first attacked from behind, perhaps while lying down. On his head and face are signs that he was set upon with clubs, maces, and axes. However, there is no evidence of any palace intrigue during his reign, and the explanation does not account fully for the poor condition of the body at the time of burial. His is the worst preserved of all the royal mummies in the Egyptian Museum.

A second explanation, that he was killed in battle, is

the one most generally accepted today. Not only are the wounds compatible with the type one would expect in such a situation (being first attacked from behind does not disprove this), but the fact that his body was very poorly embalmed and wrapped suggests that this was done some distance from Thebes, where neither time nor equipment was available for proper embalming.

One of the results of this hasty embalming was that a strong odor, a rather foul, oily smell, filled the room the moment the case in which his body was exhibited was opened. Probably natron was not used in the embalming process, so that some body fluids remained in the body after burial. The x-rays showed that no attempt had been made to remove the brain or to insert linen into the cranium or the eyes, all usual practices during this time. One can imagine Tao, fallen in battle, being carried from the field and embalmed with whatever materials were at hand before being sent south by boat to Thebes, there to be buried in a tomb hastily prepared for the unexpected funeral.

Of particular interest and importance are the physical features revealed by Tao's mummy. All the teeth, and he possesses a complete set, are remarkably healthy, well spaced, and practically unworn—none of these were particularly common attributes of the Egyptian pharaohs. His entire lower facial complex, in fact, is so different from other pharaohs (it is closest to that of his son Ahmose) that he could be fitted more easily into the series of Nubian and Old Kingdom Giza skulls than into that of later Egyptian kings. Various scholars in the past have proposed a Nubian—that is, non-Egyptian—origin for Seqenenre and his family, and his facial features suggest this might indeed be true.[1] If it is, the history of the family that reputedly drove the Hyksos from Egypt, and the history of the Seventeenth Dynasty, stand in need of considerable re-examination.

The trial transcripts of the great tomb robberies in the Twentieth Dynasty remark that the tomb of Seqenenre Tao was found intact. If that was the case, then it was not long after the inspection that his relatively inferior burial was stripped of its salable objects. A very patient group of thieves spent considerable time carefully scraping the gold from his gilded coffin, concealing the patches they laid bare with yellow paint, and adding painted substitutes for the precious stones they removed. Herbert Winlock, an American archaeologist who worked in Egypt during the 1920s, has suggested that this thievery was performed by the priests who supposedly guarded the tomb. The gold was not removed from any of the religious or royal symbols on the coffin—the royal uraeus (the sacred cobra carved on the rim of the pharaoh's crown) and the name of the god Ptah Sokar, for example —and he has convincingly argued that such devoutly inspired discrimination would only have been shown by members of the priesthood.[2]

Some years before his death Seqenenre Tao married his sister Ahhotep I, thereby strengthening the claim their children would have to the throne. This was the first of such marriages among the descendants of Tetisheri. (Consanguineous marriage was considered improper only among commoners.)

Ahhotep I, who outlived her husband by several years, was treated by later generations in the same fashion as her mother. Her sons called her "one who cares for Egypt," and she, perhaps more than anyone else, maintained the Theban court and protected its holdings from attacks by the Hyksos after her husband's sudden death. In contrast to her husband's rather simple burial, Ahhotep was interred in splendid fashion. Hoards of jewelry were found with her coffin near the entrance to the Valley of the Kings, but her mummy was so badly damaged it could not be x-rayed.

Ahhotep I and Seqenenre Tao had at least six children, of whom three survived childhood, and it was they who finally succeeded in driving the Hyksos from the Nile Valley. The first of them to follow Seqenenre Tao on the throne was Kamose, who, because of pride or perhaps of necessity, immediately embarked on a military campaign. Early in his reign he succeeded in capturing the southernmost Hyksos garrison, Nefrusy, 275 miles north of Thebes. Whether he penetrated farther into Hyksos territory is uncertain. If he did, he probably did not get very far, for there is evidence that he died not long after this initial foray against the enemy. His death, like his father's, was sudden and unexpected. How he died is not known, since his mummy was in extremely poor condition when found: it crumbled to dust in the excavator's hands.

2.

The single most important target of the Theban rulers in their battles to expel the Hyksos was the Hyksos capital, Avaris, located in the eastern delta. Ahmose I, who succeeded his brother Kamose, set the destruction of that city as his goal; as a result of his successful attack and the subsequent withdrawal of the Hyksos he was labeled the founder of Egypt's Eighteenth Dynasty by later chroniclers, even though he was not himself the founder of its royal line. One ancient historian stated that 240,-000 Hyksos left Egypt under the terms of a treaty signed following the collapse of their cities. Ahmose, during his long reign of twenty-five or thirty years, strengthened Egypt's eastern borders against future attack and, in the south, brought Nubia back under control of the Theban throne only a few years after it had attempted to declare its independence. After two hundred years of foreign domination, Upper and Lower Egypt were again united behind secure boundaries. The great cultural traditions of the Old and Middle Kingdoms could be continued and elaborated upon.

The last years of Ahmose's life, though politically and militarily successful, were very painful. X-rays have revealed that arthritis affected his knees and back, and movement must at times have been very difficult.

The mummy of Ahmose was one of those examined in the Egyptian Museum by Smith about 1912, but Smith had been unable to learn much because of the thick resinous paste with which the embalmers had coated the body. While the Michigan team was studying the mummy collection in 1970, the linen sheet covering Ahmose's body was removed to see if more features could be identified, and it was decided to take x-rays from several different angles in the hip area. These turned out to be extremely important, for they gave good evidence that this early New Kingdom ruler was uncircumcised.

Male circumcision, according to Herodotus, was universally practiced in Egypt during dynastic times, and evidence of the techniques used has been found in an Old Kingdom relief at Saqqara. It was customary for all males except some members of the lowest social classes to be circumcised at puberty, yet here was a pharaoh who clearly had not had the operation. It seemed extremely odd that the king, the representative of Egypt's cultural and religious traditions, should have been denied what was, as Herodotus suggested, a symbol of Egyptianness.

Why this was so is not known, but one cannot help wondering if this is not further confirmation of a foreign origin of the late Seventeenth-Dynasty rulers, or a confirmation of some physical disorder, perhaps inherited—hemophilia, for example—which the Egyptians realized would have made such an operation fatal. Further, Ahmose, to judge by his skeleton, was a delicately built individual, far less robust than his father or later kings, a fact that might well suggest a history of poor physical health, which made circumcision undesirable.

The thick resin with which the body was covered prevented any specific comparison between him and his predecessors, for even x-rays did not produce clear results. Nevertheless, the x-rays did suggest that Ahmose and Seqenenre Tao shared many general physical features that were strikingly different from those of later Egyptian rulers. Again, one wonders if both were not genetically influenced by peoples of the south.

Ahmose, like his father before him, married his sister. His wife, Ahmose-Nefertiry, was the third of the three great women of this period whose memory was to be perpetuated after her death and whose power perhaps explains why, four generations later, an attempt was made to establish matriarchal rule in Egypt. Even in reliefs carved during the reign of her husband she was shown in the same scale as the king and the god Amon-Re. This was an unusual mark of distinction. Upon her death, her son gave her the honor of sharing his royal mortuary temple.

The mummy of Nefertiry was also found in the Deir el-Bahri cache. Her right hand, wrenched from the arm and tossed into the coffin beside the body, attests to the cavalier fashion in which the tomb robbers of the Twentieth Dynasty had treated their victims and explains why priests were anxious to move the bodies to safer chambers. Like her grandmother, Tetisheri, she was noticeably bald and wore strands of hair twisted with her own to hide that fact. She died at an advanced age, perhaps seventy, for her torso was withered and emaciated. The marked maxillary protrusion (buck teeth) noted in the mummy of Tetisheri was even more pronounced in her granddaughter, suggesting a rather close relationship, since the tendency toward malocclusion has been considered a genetic characteristic. In addition to dentition, there was marked similarity in skeletal form.

It is interesting that Nefertiry and her brother Ahmose show little similarity in skeletal form. The differences are such, in fact, that it may be that she and Ahmose, while having the same father, had different mothers. This would not be surprising: the society of ancient Egypt was polygamous. But how solid the genealogical picture of this period really is still is open to question.

The son of Ahmose and Ahmose-Nefertiry, Amenhotep I, ascended the throne in 1546 B.C. at about twenty-five years of age, perhaps after six or seven years under his mother's regency. This date, which may be given with considerable certainty, has been established by a short inscription on the back of the famous Ebers Medical Papyrus, which records an astronomical phenomenon, the rising of the star Sirius, in the ninth year of his reign. Such astronomical occurrences can be fixed with considerable accuracy, and their mention in papyri, particularly in those of the New Kingdom, are major sources of Egyptian chronology.

As with other New Kingdom rulers, Amenhotep I and the events of his reign are known only in barest outline. He married two of his sisters, Ahhotep II and Ahmose Meryet-Amon, and during his twenty-one-year rule he continued the consolidation of Egypt and the expansion of the internal reorganization begun by his father. He also may have campaigned outside the Nile Valley and strengthened the boundaries established after the expulsion of the Hyksos and the suppression of Nubian independence.

Apparently in an attempt to conceal and protect his mummy from tomb robberies, Amenhotep I built his mortuary temple some distance from his tomb—a significant departure from the earlier practice of keeping tomb and temple together. The temple, erected on the edge of the cultivation at Thebes, was shared by his mother, and its location is known. Though modern Egyptologists have been unable to locate his tomb ancient tomb robbers did find it and probably removed all its treasures. His badly battered mummy was found in the Deir el-Bahri cache, where it had been placed after being rewrapped by priests of the Twenty-first Dynasty.

The rewrapping was so well done that Smith did not attempt to examine the mummy for fear of damage to the linen. The x-rays taken by the Michigan Expedition provided the first glimpse of that pharaoh in over three thousand years. The beautiful wrappings were extremely fragile, and there were anxious moments as the workmen carefully placed the mummy under the x-ray unit. When the body was removed from its museum case the smell of delphiniums, which had been wrapped with the mummy, was a pungent reminder of how well Egypt's dry climate preserves organic remains.

These x-rays—the first taken of a fully wrapped mummy—were not disappointing. The frontal views of the head showed the skull, chin down, with the eyes, mouth, and ears of his cartonnage (the face mask of linen and plaster) eerily superimposed. Medically he was a healthy specimen if a bit thin, with little dental wear and excellent teeth. Like his predecessors, he had a pronounced chin. On his right arm was a small amulet, and a belt of large beads was strung round his waist, probably added during the rewrapping.

The x-rays were not as conclusive as was hoped, but there seemed to be a very strong possibility that Amenhotep I, like Ahmose before him, was uncircumcised.

One of the wives-sisters of Amenhotep I, Ahmose-Meryet-Amon, was also x-rayed. She showed a pattern of dentition similar to that of her husband-brother and to that of the women of her family, Tetisheri and Nefertiry, who preceded her. The third molar was unerupted, which meant that she died early in the third decade of life. Her mummy, like that of her husband, indicated that she suffered from several physical ailments. In the vertebral column were both evidence of arthritis, which in itself could be severely uncomfortable, and marked scoliosis (an abnormal lateral curvature of the spine), which would have made movement difficult and painful. In the pelvic area a few beads, probably the remnants of pieces of jewelry taken by tomb robbers, were found.

Amenhotep I probably had several children, but his only known son, Amenemhet, died in infancy, thus leaving no heir to the throne. He therefore designated his brother-in-law, Thutmosis, to succeed him.

3.

Thutmosis I was a man of humble birth whose only claim to kingship was his marriage to two of Amenhotep's sisters, Ahmose and Mutnofret, but he proved himself more than worthy of its power. In his short reign of only ten years, the former glory of Egypt was successfully revived. Expeditions into Nubia extended Egyptian authority as far south as the Fourth Cataract, while campaigns in the east were fought even beyond the Euphrates River. At home, his additions to the Temple of Karnak added to his fame. This was only a small structure then, but it was soon to become the most impressive and important of Egypt's religious monuments.

In the year 1512 B.C., when he was supposedly about fifty years old, Thutmosis I "went to his rest from life and ascended to heaven after he had completed his years in happiness."[3] A few years after his burial his daughter Hatshepsut moved his mummy to her own mortuary structure, where it remained until his grandson restored it to its rightful burial spot in the Valley of the Kings. Thutmosis' mortuary temple has not been found, but his tomb, built by the Royal Architect Ineny, was the first royal tomb to be uncovered in the Valley of the Kings.

The mummy of Thutmosis I was in good shape even though no resinous coating had been spread over the body. The only damage, in fact, was to the hands, which had been placed over the genitals and were broken off. He was completely bald at death; his dentition was only moderately worn. X-rays of the pelvic region indicated that he, like many other Egyptian pharaohs, had to tolerate the pain of arthritis, in this case rheumatoid arthritis, and at one time he suffered a fractured pelvis. Physically he was different from his brother-in-law Amenhotep I; x-rays reinforced the historic finding that there was no direct relationship between them.

Egyptologists who have reconstructed the chronology of the Eighteenth Dynasty from textual evidence generally have assigned a reign of ten years to Thutmosis I and have assumed that he died at about the age of fifty. However, several eminent physical anthropologists who have seen these x-rays have been absolutely convinced that this mummy is that of a young man, perhaps eighteen years of age, certainly not over twenty. Such an age is simply not compatible with the chronology of this period, and there does not seem to be any convincing explanation. It is possible that the history of the period is in error, that Thutmosis I was in fact a child-king whose reign was much shorter than is supposed. But the textual basis of the chronology seems fairly solid and not likely to allow such drastic revision. It is also possible, as suggested by Smith, that the mummy labeled Thutmosis I is in fact the mummy of someone else, perhaps mistaken for the king by later priests who rewrapped his body. Or it may be the mummy of Thutmosis I, and he suffered from some disorder that delayed the normal maturation of the skeleton. Such disorders may have included those of nutritional origin (rickets), endocrinopathies (hypothyroidism), osteoporosis, and so on. It remains to be seen which of these explanations is correct. But again, x-rays have cast considerable doubt on the generally accepted reconstruction of New Kingdom history.

The striking physical difference between Thutmosis and previous kings makes one wonder if he might not have been the first New Kingdom pharaoh to lack any genetic relationship with them. As we have seen, Seqenenre Tao, Ahmose, Amenhotep I, and, to a lesser extent, their wives show far more similarity to one another than to later rulers. Thutmosis, on the other hand, shows little resemblance to them and much to his successors. His reign may well mark a genetic turning point in the Egyptian royal line.

The chief wife of Thutmosis I, Ahmose, bore two sons and a daughter. The sons did not survive their father, and the throne passed to Thutmosis II, a son born of his second wife Mutnofret. Thutmosis II was a sickly man who died after a reign of only eight years.

His mummy was badly hacked up by ancient tomb robbers in their search for gold amulets inside the wrappings. But enough has remained, particularly of the skull and teeth, to show that there was such a close resemblance between him and Thutmosis I that they seem almost like twin brothers rather than father and son.

Examination of the teeth shows that Thutmosis II died at an early age, probably around thirty. His skin was covered by a number of scabrous patches, and he appears to have been a frail individual. Most writers have agreed that these features are indicative of disease, perhaps the disease from which he died, but as yet no examination of the soft tissue has been possible and the disease remains unidentified.

During the reign of Thutmosis II the army conducted expeditions in the south, where they crushed a Nubian revolt; and in the east, where a Bedouin uprising was put down. Yet his control of the throne was weak, perhaps because of poor health. To strengthen his claim to power, he married his half-sister Hatshepsut, the daughter of Ahmose and Thutmosis I. In doing so he was to change the course of Egyptian history.

It is not known if Thutmosis II was aware of Hatshepsut's ambitions and desire for power, but it may have been as a result of her machinations that he took pains to insure that his son, Thutmosis III, born to a minor concubine named Isis, be made king upon his death. It is likely that his son was proclaimed co-regent near the end of his reign to guarantee that succession.

Thutmosis III was still a young child when his father died, and Hatshepsut "conducted the affairs of the country, the Two Lands being in her control. People worked for her, and Egypt bowed [its] head."[4] At first, Hatshepsut played only the role of regent; but during the second year of her stepson's reign she took over all authority from the young ruler and was crowned King of Upper and Lower Egypt.*

Hatshepsut is an enigmatic and poorly understood figure in Egyptian history, and the reconstruction of events during her reign and leading up to it is still unclear. Even the chronology and sequence of rulers during the Eighteenth Dynasty are difficult to piece together, and the problem of the so-called Thutmosid Succession is not yet resolved to the satisfaction of every scholar. The historical fictions perpetrated by Hatshepsut and her cohort, the Chief Steward Senenmut, do not help to clarify the situation. In texts and inscriptions, she claimed divine birth and maintained that her father had crowned her king in the presence of the court, implying that her stepson had less right to the throne than she. To strengthen these claims she even ordered the body of her father, Thutmosis I, moved to her own tomb.

On the basis of Hatshepsut's activities and inscriptions, and the way in which the names of many kings were scratched out and other names inserted, early Egyptologists reconstructed a series of coups and countercoups for this period of the Eighteenth Dynasty, trying to show the ways in which Hatshepsut and her successors vied for power. Their list suggests a game of

*The Egyptians had no word equivalent to "queen" in the modern sense; hence Hatsheput, when she assumed royal authority, had to be called "king." When the word queen occurs later in this book, it is used to denote the wife of a king; these "queens" did not rule in their own right. However, in the late New Kingdom a king's wife frequently was also the high priestess of Amon, with power equal to or greater than that of the king.

THE PHARAOH'S MUMMY

musical chairs, and most modern scholars have disagreed with these findings.

Donald Redford, a modern Canadian Egyptologist, who has re-examined the problems of this period, believes Hatshepsut's attainment of the throne represents the final attempt in the Eighteenth Dynasty to establish a strong matriarchate in Egypt. He cites the unusual importance of earlier queens in this period—Tetisheri, Ahhotep I, Ahmose-Nefertiry—as evidence of such a tendency, and he suggests that the influences for such a matriarchally determined order of succession might have come from Nubia.[5] The possibility that the rulers of the Seventeenth Dynasty were themselves at least part Nubian has already been mentioned.

Whatever the reason for Hatshepsut's rise to power, she remained in control of Egypt for twenty-one years, nineteen of them as king. Under her leadership Egypt conducted only minor military campaigns; instead, much of its energy was devoted to building, exploration, and trade.

Hatshepsut had a large tomb carved for herself. It was carefully hidden, 230 feet above the valley floor, in cliffs a mile west of her temple at Deir el-Bahri. It is unlikely that she was buried there, however, for the tomb was found to be empty and only partly finished.

The mummy of Hatshepsut has not yet been identified with certainty. Some members of the Michigan Expedition have wondered if the mummy of an "elder woman" (number CGC 61070) found in the tomb of Amenhotep II might not in fact be her remains. There are several reasons for this belief. In terms of the techniques of mummification this individual exhibits, it is certain that she was embalmed during this period of the Eighteenth Dynasty. The approximate age of the mummy at death

—about thirty-five to forty-five—fits what we know of the length of Hatshepsut's life. Physically she bears a strong resemblance to the mummies of Thutmosis II and III. The left arm of the mummy (the only arm visible at the present time) is flexed and lies over the chest with the fist clenched. The position suggests that she might have been buried holding one of the symbols of royal office (see the hands of the mummy of Thutmosis IV). Finally, her burial in the tomb of Amenhotep II, along with kings and nobles of the New Kingdom, suggests that she, too, was at least of the nobility, if not of the royal family itself.

This mummy has not yet been x-rayed. It is hoped that the head, which is undamaged and still covered by long curls of brown hair, will reveal enough specific similarities to the Thutmosid pharaohs to confirm this tentative identification.

4.

After twenty-two years spent in the shadow of Hatshepsut, Thutmosis III finally achieved independent power at her death, presumably from natural causes, in 1469 B.C. He may not have mourned the loss of his domineering stepmother, but modern scholars do not believe he engaged in the vindictive destruction of her monuments some have ascribed to him. There were other, more urgent demands of state, for Hatshepsut's reign, though by no means as pacific as some historians have maintained, saw only small-scale military exploits to preserve Egypt's foreign holdings. Thutmosis III was quickly forced to turn to strengthening the empire. In his military ventures as well as in his many domestic affairs, he was to earn a reputation as Egypt's greatest and most powerful ruler.

Thutmosis III had his tomb carved in the Valley of the Kings, following the basic design used by all the Thutmosid pharaohs. His mummy was presumably removed from here in the Twenty-second Dynasty and hidden in the Deir el-Bahri cache. It was found, badly damaged by plunderers, in a state hardly fitting Egypt's greatest ruler.

William Hayes, late Curator of the Department of Egyptian Art at the Metropolitan Museum in New York, has described Thutmosis III as a "Napoleonic little man who appears to have excelled not only as a general, a statesman, and an administrator, but also as one of the most accomplished horsemen, archers and all-round athletes of his time."[6] Certainly everything known about him justifies such praises.

Barely five feet tall and of medium build, the mummy of Thutmosis III is similar to those of Thutmosis I and II and to that of his son, Amenhotep II. The teeth are well spaced, and although they show some wear there are neither caries nor any of the dental problems common to later rulers. On his right arm he wears a wide bracelet and a twist of wire, the latter probably added by later restorers, who had also to resort to narrow wooden splints to hold parts of the badly damaged mummy together. The incision made in the abdomen for removal of the viscera is relatively small (about four inches long), well made, and carefully stitched closed.

Like all the pharaohs, Thutmosis III had several wives and numerous concubines. His Great Wife was Meryetre-Hatshepsut, about whom almost nothing is known except that she, and not another of his wives (his half-sister), was the mother of his son Amenhotep II. (It is not likely that she was related to Hatshepsut.)

Thutmosis III died after fifty-five years as king, on

March 17, 1436 B.C., according to Hayes' calculations, although the x-rays do not support such an advanced age.[7] Presumably he had been ailing for some time, since two years and four months before his death he appointed his son co-regent to assure his accession to the throne.

On the morning of March 18, Amenhotep II became king. Eighteen years old at the time, he was taller than most of Egypt's rulers, muscular, and an extremely able athlete. Like his father, he boasted of his talents as archer, horseman, hunter, and soldier.

Amenhotep II pursued the military goals that his father had set, waging bloody but successful battles in Syria and pushing the limits of Egypt's control in the Sudan as far south as the Fourth Cataract, nearly eight hundred miles upstream from Aswan. At home, he erected numerous temples and shrines, added to the Temple of Amon at Karnak, and generously supported the arts. Again like his father, his activities were numerous and catholic, and Egypt during his reign stood supreme in the world.

The tomb that Amenhotep II had carved for himself in the Valley of the Kings is similar to most other royal tombs of this period, but its contents give it special distinction: it is one of the very few royal tombs found with the original owner's mummy still present and intact.

Although taller than both his father and his son, Amenhotep II bore a marked resemblance to both of them, especially to Thutmosis IV, particularly in respect to their crania and teeth. His wavy hair was brown with gray at the temple, and there was a small bald spot at the back of his head. He must have been about forty-five years old when he died. The x-rays showed evidence of rheumatoid arthritis, but this inflammation and degeneration of the vertebral column had not advanced to a particularly severe stage. On his neck, shoulders, thorax, and abdomen were small nodules, probably the results of some systemic disease. Since a tissue sample of the mummy was not obtainable their exact cause could not be determined.

Amenhotep II was succeeded by his son, Thutmosis IV. Between the paws of the Great Sphinx at Giza, Thutmosis IV erected a granite stela on which he described how he became king. While resting one day at Giza, he relates, the god Harmakhis came to him in a dream, promising him power and wealth and the throne of Egypt if he would clear the sand away from the huge image with which the god was identified. "The sands of the desert, which once I had been upon now are upon me. [But] I have waited to let you do what was in my heart. . . ."[8]

Thutmosis did remove the sand from the Sphinx, but, the oracle notwithstanding, he became king of Upper and Lower Egypt because, as the son of Amenhotep II, he was the rightful heir. He ascended the throne in 1425 B.C. and, according to the ancient historian Josephus, ruled for nine years and eight months.

The mummy of Thutmosis IV is that of an extremely emaciated man, slightly bald, who died at only thirty years of age. Although nothing can be learned about the cause of this emaciated condition since that would require the removal of tissue samples, it seems likely that, whatever the disease, it contributed to his death. The dehydrating effects of the mummification process cannot fully account for his present condition.

In spite of his illness Thutmosis IV bears a considerable resemblance to Amenhotep II, a fact that helps confirm the known order of royal succession.

The well-manicured fingernails and carefully pierced ears show him to have been well cared for before death, but the large and rather crude incision made in the abdomen by the embalmers suggests a hasty and even rather unprofessional job of mummification. The heart, left in the body as was customary at this time, can be seen in the x-ray, slightly displaced to the right. The hands are crossed over the chest, and the fingers still curve around the now-missing flail and scepter, symbols of the pharaoh's power and authority.

From the marriage of Thutmosis IV and Mutemwiya came a son, Amenhotep III, who ascended the throne upon his father's death in 1417 B.C. During the years of Thutmosid rule in Egypt, the country's economic and military successes had made it the most powerful force in the ancient world, and Amenhotep III was able to devote himself to the consumption of the goods brought from its vast empire rather than to further military raids. This he did with considerable energy and remarkably good taste. The large number of monuments he erected, particularly the Temple of Amon at Luxor, the additions to the Temple at Karnak, and his own palace, the Malkata, are among the the most splendid examples of New Kingdom architecture. The statuary, painting, and minor arts of his reign are second to none, in large part because officials of his court played a prominent role as patrons. Their acquired wealth also enabled them to devote much care to their own funerary preparations.

Early in his reign Amenhotep III took as his wife a woman named Tiy, the daughter of two lesser officials at the court. Her father was Yuya, the king's Lieutenant of Chariotry and Master of the Horses; Thuya, her mother, was called the Royal Ornament, probably signifying her role as lady-in-waiting.

Egyptologists have attributed to Tiy a number of characteristics. Some have seen in her features a demanding and perhaps even vicious woman, others simply a foreign background. Neither view is correct; but it is likely that she played a significant role in the policies of her husband and worked closely with him and his numerous officials in the administration of Egypt.

Tiy's parents, although not of royal lineage, did achieve considerable authority and wealth thanks to their daughter's marriage. Their tomb, discovered in 1905 in a small spur of the Valley of the Kings, yielded a number of important objects even though it had been heavily plundered in ancient times.

Particularly interesting are the mummies of Yuya and Thuya, two of the most striking and beautifully preserved mummies known from ancient Egypt. Both have long reddish-blond hair and, with their carefully restored facial features, give an astonishingly lifelike appearance. Their wrappings are well preserved, and both are covered with decorated strips of linen soaked in a solution of thin plaster.

A considerable amount of gold still remains on the bodies. Lying upon the incision in Yuya's abdomen, under the wrappings, is a gold plate affixed with resin, used to seal the wound. Yuya still wears rings on his fingers. Evidence of marked degenerative arthritis may be seen in x-rays of the vertebrae and knees.

Fewer funerary objects were found in the body of Thuya, but a large tubular bead was revealed near the left thigh.

In spite of their attractive appearance both suffered from bad dentition—the worst of all but one of the mummies studied (that one was Ramesses II). Missing teeth, heavy wear, and evidence of abscesses were found in both. Thuya also suffered from arthritis, and scoliosis may be seen in the upper part of her back.

Yuya and Thuya were not embalmed by the same technique, for the former clearly shows evidence of the bones of the nose having been broken to extract the brain and of linen and resin packing having been inserted in the cranium. Thuya shows neither of these features; the brain apparently was not removed. The most likely explanation of this difference is that husband and wife died at different times and different embalmers were responsible for preparing their bodies. Perhaps this is an indication that the techniques of mummification were less uniform during various periods of the New Kingdom than has generally been believed.

When the mummy of Amenhotep III was found in the cache hidden in the tomb of his grandfather Amenhotep II, it was so badly damaged that even his age at death was difficult to determine. Smith estimated that Amenhotep III died between forty and fifty years of age, probably in 1379 B.C. Since he reigned for just over thirty-eight years, the latter figure, fifty years, is more nearly correct. At any rate, the mummy does show that Amenhotep III spent the last years of his life as a fat, diseased, sedentary man, almost completely bald, who doubtless was in considerable pain from dental problems. It may have been to ease his pain, in fact, that King Tushratta of Babylonia sent him a statuette of the goddess Ishtar, widely believed to possess healing powers.

Like Yuya and Thuya, Amenhotep III had bad teeth, considerably worn, with heavy tartar deposits and evidence of abscesses. It seems possible that the Egyptians at the royal court had a richer and more varied diet than did the fellahin; however, their major dental problems appear to have been remarkably similar.

More interesting than pathology, however, is the technique of mummification used in preparing this king for burial. When unwrapping the badly damaged body, Smith noted numerous attempts to restore a lifelike appearance to the limbs. Resin and bits of linen had been placed in the mouth and under the skin of the legs, arms, and neck, and then molded to the proper form. The resinous material turned out to be radiopaque, and clear x-rays could not be obtained.

It is worth noting that the mummy of Amenhotep III shows absolutely no sign of the unusual physical attributes commonly associated with his son, Amenhotep IV.

✣ 5.

No pharaoh of ancient Egypt has been the subject of more discussion and more varied explanation than Amenhotep IV. During his reign he abandoned the traditional capital of Egypt, Thebes, and moved to a new city, Akhetaton—or Tell el-Amarna, as it is also called (hence the name "the Amarna Period"). He pushed Egypt's many traditional gods into the background and elevated a single, and formerly minor deity, Aton, to prominence.

In the art of this period the king is depicted by an unconventional figure, a man with narrow shoulders and broad hips, feminine breasts and an emaciated face, a family man frequently shown with his daughters and wife in poses of very un-Egyptian informality. He has been called the world's first monotheist, an independent and revolutionary philosopher, a mentally corrupt pacifist, a helpless victim of severe glandular disorders. These are overstatements; but there is no doubt that his actions and beliefs brought about major changes in traditional

Egyptian culture and that he suffered from some pathological condition.

His brother Thutmosis, who ordinarily would have inherited the throne, had died in infancy, and Amenhotep IV was made co-regent with his father about 1385 B.C. He was perhaps sixteen years old at the time, and shortly thereafter he took his maternal first cousin, Nefertity, as his wife.

It was some time after his father's death that the young king abandoned Thebes and constructed an entirely new capital city about halfway between Luxor and Cairo. He changed his name from Amenhotep ("Amon is Content") to Akhenaton ("One who is Serviceable to Aton"), and at Karnak, the stronghold of the god Amon, he built a temple to Aton. These actions must have led to discontent among the priests of other temples, who suddenly found the offerings formerly given to them diverted to serve the new god, but there is no evidence that such discontent ever manifested itself in insurrection or, as some suggest, in the violent defacement of Akhenaton's memory immediately after his death. Most of the destruction of his temples and inscriptions took place some years later, and succeeding kings of the Eighteenth Dynasty simply ignored the Amarna religion and its founder.

Akhenaton's peculiar physical condition has engendered intense debate. The most generally accepted explanation is that he suffered from what is known as Fröhlich's syndrome (adiposogenital dystrophy). Its most striking effects are excessive fatty deposits, particularly in the pelvic region, and lack of development of sex organs and of secondary sex characteristics, such as body hair and changes in voice.

Though these symptoms of Fröhlich's syndrome seem

to fit Akhenaton's condition, the diagnosis still poses problems. The changes described manifest themselves at the time of puberty; yet the early representations of Akhenaton show him in no way different from the norm of other Egyptian royal figures. An ostracon (an informal drawing on a stone fragment) from later in Akhenaton's reign shows him with an unshaven face as a sign of mourning. Facial hair should not appear on victims of Fröhlich's syndrome. Further, it is difficult to reconcile the inability to reproduce caused by the syndrome with the fact that Akhenaton describes himself as the father of six daughters and husband to not a few wives. Cyril Aldred, an eminent Egyptologist particularly concerned with this period, has raised the possibility that Akhenaton was not the biological father of these girls—that Amenhotep III had filled that role.[9] Other scholars have noted that Akhenaton appears in some scenes in unusually friendly poses with Smenkhare, his successor to the throne. The French Egyptologist Georges Lefebvre even saw in a cryptic reference by the ancient historian Manetho to Amenhotep III and "his daughter Acencheres"[10] a hint that Akhenaton had masqueraded as a woman and was a transvestite. Another French Egyptologist, Auguste Mariette (1821–1881), the man who was instrumental in founding the Egyptian Museum, thought that Akhenaton had been castrated while on a military expedition in the Sudan.

The answer to these problems was thought to have been found in 1907, when a mummy was uncovered in tomb No. 55 in the Valley of the Kings. The body lay in the coffin originally made for Akhenaton's daughter Meryet-Amon. The excavator, Theodore Davis, an American lawyer and amateur Egyptologist, was at first convinced that the body was that of Queen Tiy, and, according to Davis, several physicians, whom he did not identify, supported that conclusion. Later medical studies by Smith showed that the body was clearly that of a young man, twenty to twenty-five years old, and many Egyptologists immediately concluded that it was the mummy of Akhenaton. This identification, based on the grave goods, has been shown to be extremely tenuous. Both Aldred and R.G. Harrison, professor of anatomy at the University of Liverpool, having re-examined all the material in 1966, convincingly argue that the body is that of Smenkhare, Akhenaton's successor and nephew.[11] The only evidence left to help solve the problem of Akhenaton is the art and inscriptions of the Amarna Period, and clearly that alone is not enough. The real nature of the illness suffered by the man who so altered Egyptian religion during his lifetime remains a mystery.

After ruling for sixteen years, Akhenaton took Smenkhare, his nephew and son-in-law, as co-regent. The events that led up to this are unclear. It is known that Smenkhare's wife, Meryet-Amon, was Akhenaton's favorite daughter, whom Akhenaton himself had married some years before his death. For unexplained reasons Nefertity, Akhenaton's Great Wife, mysteriously disappears from the texts and reliefs of the period, suggesting that she had fallen from favor. It is also known that there was a close friendship between Akhenaton and Smenkhare. Whether any or all of these are the reasons, Smenkhare ruled for about two years as co-regent and alone after Akhenaton's death for slightly more than one.

The human remains once thought to be those of Akhenaton and now considered those of Smenkhare are in a very sorry state of preservation: only an incomplete skeleton and broken skull remain. But these scanty remains reveal a man who resembles the Thutmosid line, whose unworn teeth are those of a young man, and whose skeleton offers no positive evidence of any physical ailment (a tentative diagnosis of hydrocephalus is still highly tenuous, and x-rays do not support it).

Shortly after Smenkhare became ruler of Egypt, Nefertity seems to have made a comeback. There is correspondence between her and a Hittite king, asking for his son in marriage, so that he might serve as Egypt's ruler. References to Smenkhare and Meryet-Amon suddenly disappear. A plot to gain control of the throne may well have been underway, although the evidence is too meager to be certain of its character. However, it was Nefertity who managed the events that, in 1361 B.C., made Tutankhaton king.

Tutankhaton, the brother of Smenkhare, was only nine or ten years old at his accession, and he remained with Nefertity and her father Ay at Akhetaton.

Probably at the behest of Nefertity, the young Tutankhaton took Nefertity's daughter Ankh-es-en-pa-aton as his wife.

They ruled under the direction of Ay and Nefertity for three years, loyal to the Aton in spite of the relapse into orthodoxy, which had surfaced in the later years of Akhenaton's reign. This loyalty was not to last. Smenkhare had already made strong moves to reassert the power of Thebes and its temples. In the fourth year of his reign Tutankhaton moved the royal court back to the former capital. Shortly thereafter he changed his name from Tutankhaton to Tutankhamon and embarked on an ambitious restoration of the temples of Amon and their substantial properties.

It is ironic that such a young ruler, whose power was so completely in the hands of his advisers, and who died after only nine years on the throne before reaching the age of twenty, should be the Egyptian ruler most people today associate with Egypt's opulence and power. This, of course, is due to the famous discovery of "King Tut's Tomb" by Howard Carter and Lord Carnarvon in 1922 —one of the very few unplundered tombs known from Egypt and by any standard a collection of incredible wealth.

The mummy of Tutankhamon, which still lies in his tomb in the Valley of the Kings, has not yet been x-rayed by the Michigan Expedition. X-rays taken recently by another expedition have revealed no major pathological conditions.[12] The body, though damaged, seems to fit well with other royal mummies of this period, though the x-rays taken were not so aligned that any useful comparisons are possible. A recent attempt to determine Tutankhamon's blood type from the chemical analysis of bone gives further—though not definite—proof of his relationship to Smenkhare.[13]

When Tutankhamon died in 1352 B.C. he left no heir to the throne, no one to continue the family line of the Thutmosid rulers. Several members of the court attempted to establish themselves as king. His wife, Ankh-es-en-Amon (Ankh-es-en-pa-aton before changing her name), went so far as to try again what her mother had unsuccessfully attempted: she wrote the Hittite king to send one of his sons to serve as her husband and become king of Egypt. This time the plan almost succeeded. But before the young prince could arrive at the court, her plan was discovered (perhaps by the General of the Army, Horemhab), and he was assassinated. As a result, Ankh-es-en-Amon wed her own grandfather, Ay, and he was duly installed as pharaoh.

It was a futile attempt to maintain the family line, for

Ay was an old man and his reign lasted only four years. Upon his death, Horemhab, who had served as general under Akhenaton and Tutankhamon and who even wrote that he had acted as vice-regent for many years, was declared ruler.

In spite of Horemhab's earlier allegiance to Akhenaton, his first act was the systematic destruction of the remains of the Amarna Period and its religion, including the complete sacking of Akhetaton. He did much to restore the priests of Amon to power, and he returned to their temples the offerings they had been denied by the Atonists. Only in the art style of his reign were there remnants of the Amarna Period.

His actions were undoubtedly political. Following the death of Akhenaton, Egypt was a country in turmoil, with no real leadership and little ability to maintain law and order. To stem the rise in administrative inefficiency he began restoring authority not only to the priests but to officials whose roles had been assumed by the now discredited Atonists. By strengthening the priesthood and the government bureaucracy, Horemhab was assuring Egypt's return to its traditional and—he must have hoped—formerly stable ways.

Horemhab ruled for twenty-eight years, and with his death the Eighteenth Dynasty came to an end. Neither his mummy nor that of Ay has been found.

FIVE ✝ THE MORTAL MUMMY
—Examination of Kings and Priests

The next three dynasties saw a steady decline in Egypt's position, only rarely interspersed with short periods of relative stability and partial recovery. Toward the end of Ramesside rule there were ominous indications of trouble. Militarily, there were large incursions of foreigners into the Nile Valley. Diplomatically, foreign rulers showed their disrespect. Economically, Egypt made desperate attempts to acquire essential foreign goods. Tomb robbing was flagrant and the administration dishonest.

Even more threatening to royal authority was the gradually increasing role played by the priests of Amon in the affairs of state. In the Twenty-first Dynasty the priests became more powerful than the king himself, and from that point on our story will be of x-raying priests, not pharaohs.

1.

Horemhab, having no heir to follow him on the throne, had chosen to succeed him a man of humble birth from the eastern Delta, an old military compatriot, whom he already had made vizier. After the coronation this new king changed his name from Pramesse to Ramesses, and he is identified today as the first of that long line of Egyptian rulers.

Ramesses I must have been an elderly man at the time of his accession in 1320 B.C. and he ruled less than two years. During his short reign he continued to solidify the position of the throne and strengthened even more the powers of the priesthood and the growing bureaucracy. By the time of his death Egypt was internally stable and relatively prosperous.

In this new and apparently tranquil setting, Seti I, son of Ramesses I and his wife Sitre, was able to devote much of his energy to external rather than internal affairs. The years of military and diplomatic inactivity had taken their toll of Egypt's authority and wealth, and Seti, who called himself the "Repeater of Births," the leader of a renaissance, saw as his objective the restoration of Egypt's international power. In his fourteen-year reign he re-established Egypt's military control in a large part of its former territory.

At home, Seti I continued to maintain Thebes as the royal capital, and he devoted much of his time to propitiating the Theban god Amon, restoring and enlarging that god's temples and making sizable contributions of land and goods to the priesthood. But his work for Amon was not motivated solely by religious zeal.

Seti clearly was aware that the power of Amon already

was a political force to be treated carefully and well. The history of the next several centuries is a history of Amon's ever-increasing control of Egypt's resources and destiny.

Seti traced his family origins to the eastern delta, where the god Seth, an arch-rival of Amon, was supreme. At Abydos, the king showed his continued devotion to Seth by carving for him a unique subterranean chamber.

The tomb that Seti I had carved for himself is one of the most spectacular in the Valley of the Kings. A huge structure, cut 328 feet into the valley walls, its fourteen large chambers are brilliantly decorated with funerary scenes and religious texts designed to protect the king in the afterlife. Changes were taking place in Egyptian beliefs by the beginning of the Nineteenth Dynasty, and these scenes reflect an ever-increasing dependence upon religious amulets and magical incantations. John A. Wilson, the American Egyptologist who was head of the Oriental Institute at the University of Chicago for many years, attributes it to the insecurity of the post-Amarna period and to the popular belief that "man was no longer strong enough in himself" to overcome the many obstacles the gods placed in his path.[1] However efficacious prayers may have been, they did not prevent the thorough plundering of Seti's tomb and the need to hide his mummy in the Deir el-Bahri cache for protection. The mummy was found with the head and neck broken from the body, so cavalierly had the ancient plunderers treated his remains. Still, x-rays revealed a careful job of mummification. Some of the beads from an object buried with him, an Eye of Horus,* and a small

*The eye of the god Horus was originally identified with both the sun and the moon. Later, with the rise to prominence of the sun god Re, it came

fragment with geometric designs were found in the wrappings—apparently later priests gathered any material lying near the plundered mummy and included it in the rewrapped body. The king's arms were crossed over his chest in the manner of several earlier rulers, but surprisingly his hands were open, not clenched. If the flail and scepter of his office had been buried with him they had simply been placed on the body—he had not held them.

Seti's teeth were moderately worn, and one of his mandibular first molars was missing, fallen out in life, causing the second premolar to tip out of position. His heart, left in the body as was customary at this time, lay on the right side of the chest, probably displaced by the embalmers.

Seti's successor was his son, Ramesses II, often called Ramesses the Great. No pharaoh of ancient Egypt engaged in more obvious self-aggrandizement, erected more temples and shrines, or described his military exploits in greater detail. No pharaoh boasted of having more children (over one hundred sons), and few indeed reigned as many years (sixty-seven).

Ramesses II came to the throne in 1304 B.C., after some years as his father's co-regent. "He was a brash young man of about twenty, not overburdened with intelligence and singularly lacking in taste."[2] During the early years of his reign he undertook a series of military

---

to be identified as the lunar eye. In the rich mythology surrounding Horus and his brother Seth, Seth took the eye during a fight and threw it away. Later the god Thoth found it and restored it to its proper form. The name of this eye, *wadjet*, can mean "that which is sound" in Egyptian, and representations of the *wadjet*-eye came to be among the most popular amulets of ancient times. As a powerful protective amulet, it is frequently found represented on the wrappings and coffins of dynastic times.

campaigns in Western Asia, some of which successfully insured Egypt's power in the ancient world, all of which were proudly proclaimed as mighty victories by the young king. Throughout Egypt and the northern Sudan, he erected new temples and shrines or usurped those of his predecessors, decorating them with scenes and tales of his military genius and divine and human goodness.

These temples are among the largest monuments in Egypt. The great Hypostyle Hall at Karnak, which had been begun by his father, was completed during his reign and boasted 134 columns nearly thirty feet in circumference and forty-five to eighty feet in height. In Nubia, Abu Simbel was carved from the face of a huge cliff, with four colossal figures of the king guarding its entrance. In all his works size alone was the criterion of design, and all showed a severe decline in the quality of workmanship, decoration, and good taste.

The reign of Ramesses II was a period of prosperity and of relative stability. But the old traditions and ideals of past dynasties were at this time a superficial covering upon a society that was in fact very much different from that of even thirty years before.

The transfer of the Egyptian capital from Thebes to the eastern delta had been begun by Seti I and was completed under Ramesses II. The move was due to a number of factors, among which the increasingly international outlook of Egypt and the changes in religion and culture were foremost. In succeeding dynasties the effects of this move were to prove extremely serious, for it removed one of the major obstacles to the usurpation of royal powers by the priesthood of Amon.

Though Thebes was no longer the capital, the Ramesside rulers continued to be buried in the Valley of the Kings. Ramesses II had his tomb carved there. It was larger than his father's, but poorly decorated, in an ill-chosen and badly engineered site. His tomb is closed today because of its dangerously crumbling condition.

X-rays of Ramesses II and his successor, Merenptah, show considerable similarity in dentition, and both are similar to Seti I. The large noses of all three, made more dramatic by embalmer's packing, also show a close relationship between them. Ramesses II suffered from heavy dental wear and from what must have been painful alveolar abscesses, clearly visible in the x-rays. For some reason, Smith failed to note these major dental problems in his examination of the mummy. His description of Ramesses II as a man having "healthy and only slightly worn teeth" is completely erroneous.[3] Several of the teeth are loose in their sockets, and the heavy pitting of the bone around them shows this to have been a condition that developed during life. In spite of these major dental problems, Ramesses II and Seti I both show well-spaced and properly aligned dentition with none of the protrusion of the incisors characteristic of many earlier Egyptian rulers. Good dental hygiene would have saved both rulers considerable discomfort.

Ramesses II must also have been plagued by cold feet: x-rays show severe degenerative arthritis in the hip joint and arteriosclerosis of all the major arteries of the lower extremities. Such disorders often produce uncomfortable circulatory problems and make movement painful.

The superficiality and transience of the glory Ramesses II claimed to have brought Egypt is nowhere better summarized than in Shelley's poem "Ozymandias." Ramesses II, whose throne name, User-maat-Re, was heard as Ozymandias, erected a sixty-foot-high, thousand-ton statue of himself in his temple at western Thebes called the Ramesseum. Of that statue Shelley wrote:

I met a traveller from an antique land
Who said: Two vast and trunkless legs of stone
Stand in the desert. Near them on the sand
Half sunk, a shatter'd visage lies . . .

                    .   .   .

And on the pedestal these words appear:
"My name is Ozymandias, king of kings:
Look on my works, ye Mighty, and despair!"
Nothing beside remains. Round the decay
Of that colossal wreck, boundless and bare,
The lone and level sands stretch far away.

When Ramesses II died in 1237 B.C., he had outlived twelve of his hundred sons. It was his thirteenth son, Merenptah, who was crowned pharaoh.

Merenptah must have been over fifty years old when he assumed the throne, and he inherited a difficult job. The later years of his father's reign were marked by military inactivity, and his father's old age brought with it a neglect of Egypt's frontiers and defenses. His first acts, therefore, were to regain control of the deserts already overrun by Egypt's enemies, particularly the Libyans, who were being driven to attack the Nile Valley because of famine in their own country. In this he succeeded; but it was clear that Egypt's continued mastery of the military situation in North Africa and Western Asia was at best precarious. At home, his reign of only about twelve years saw little new construction, and the impression was that Egypt was on the decline.

Merenptah's tomb was perhaps his most impressive monument. His funerary temple at Thebes was built largely with fragments of other buildings, dismantled and reused here to save labor costs; but his tomb in the Valley of the Kings was one of the largest and best endowed, with painted decoration of comparatively good quality.

His mummy was found in the tomb of Amenhotep II, and it shows him an old man, partially bald and corpulent. Few royal mummies have shown so clearly the desirability of x-ray studies, for few rulers suffered so many pathological conditions, almost all of which would otherwise be invisible without careful dissection. The cervical vertebrae show severe degenerative arthritis; in the soft tissues of the thigh is evidence of arteriosclerosis; there are signs of fractures in the heads of the femurs (the thigh bones); and there is a hole (made after death?) in the right side of the cranium.

The body was badly treated by tomb robbers. An ax or knife, driven through the shoulder, split the right clavicle. The right arm was wrenched from place, and an enormous hole was hacked through the abdomen.

Curiously, the scrotum of Merenptah is completely missing, and the exposed flesh is covered with resin. Merenptah must have been castrated either shortly before death—though this is extremely unlikely—or during the embalming process, for reasons that can only be guessed.

Merenptah is believed to have been the pharaoh of the Exodus, and the heavy incrustation of salt on his skin has led some writers to claim that he was drowned in the Red Sea. Such a belief, of course, is certainly erroneous. The natron in which mummies were placed easily accounts for the salt on the body.

Like his father, Merenptah suffered from extremely poor dentition. The few remaining teeth show only moderate wear, but all the molars and premolars have been lost, and there is considerable evidence of bone loss and of periodontal disease. In examining the areas of missing teeth, particularly in the maxilla, several dentists have wondered if they might not have been deliberately removed, not just fallen out. If they were extracted, they provide almost the only evidence from dynastic Egypt of dental surgery.

From Merenptah's death in 1223 B.C. to the end of the Nineteenth Dynasty some twenty-four years later, Egypt was ruled by at least four kings. Very little is known about them: their reigns were short, the records they left vague and incomplete, and even the order in which they ruled is unclear.

It is likely that Merenptah's son, Seti II, assumed the throne on his father's death, although some scholars have proposed the intervening rule of another king, Amenmesses. Seti II ruled for six years; in regard to his activities, there is only a vague reference to a war in which he possibly took part and to a few minor additions to temples that he directed. The only document preserved in any detail, in fact, is a record of the arrest and punishment of a workman named Paneb, who was caught stealing blocks of stone from the pharaoh's tomb to use in his own mortuary structure and, worse, attempted to murder a former friend and teacher in an effort to hide that fact.

The tomb of Seti II has survived in spite of those minor thefts. It is a fairly well decorated structure in the Valley of the Kings. Throughout, the king's names have been erased, perhaps by Amenmesses or by a later ruler.

Seti II bears only slight resemblance to his father and grandfather; his face is convex, and his upper teeth protrude much more markedly. Surprisingly, his dentition is in fairly good condition; except for slight wear and a bit of crowding in the incisor region, it is perfectly healthy. Unlike his father, he suffered nothing more than slight arthritis in the hip joint. He was carefully embalmed—almost thirty long strips of bandage were used in the wrapping—but he suffered as much as any pharaoh at the hands of plunderers, who broke off the head and arms and apparently pierced the skull in their search for treasure.

When he died, Seti II had already outlived what some believe to have been his only legitimate heir to the throne. His successor was a young boy, Siptah, whose parentage is very much in doubt. Some maintain that he was not related to the royal line at all but had been placed on the throne by Seti's wife Tawosret and his chancellor, a man named Bay, as a means of gaining power for themselves. Others suggest that he was an offspring of Seti II, but by a very minor wife or concubine; still others that he was a son of Tawosret by a man other than the king. Whatever Siptah's origins, he ascended the throne in 1209 B.C. as a minor, with Tawosret and Bay in actual control of the country. He died seven years later.

His mummy, found in the Amenhotep II cache, is particularly interesting from a medical standpoint because of the severe deformity from which he suffered. His left foot has generally been diagnosed as a clubfoot. But Dr. Walter Whitehouse, the radiologist on the Michigan Expedition, has pointed out that the over-all shortening of the entire right leg and the atrophy of the soft tissues indicate the presence of a neuro-muscular disease in childhood. One disorder that generally produces such results is poliomyelitis. Polio has been identified only once before in dynastic Egypt, and then very tentatively, in a relief carving of late date, and this possible diagnosis was one of the major findings of the expedition.

Siptah's teeth are in good condition and show that he

died in his late teens or early twenties. The question of his parentage has not been solved by x-ray examination, but there is no doubt that he shows less similarity to earlier rulers than one would hope for to confirm direct genealogical relationship.

In a papyrus dated some thirty years after Siptah's death, Ramesses III wrote of the conditions under which Egypt suffered before the rise of the Twentieth Dynasty:

> The land of Egypt was cast adrift, every man a law unto himself . . . one man slaying his fellow both high and low. Then another time came after it consisting of empty years, when Irsu, a Syrian, was with them as prince, and he put the entire land in subjugation before him.[4]

Siptah was followed on the throne by Queen Tawosret herself, who reigned for about two years, with Chancellor Bay playing a major role in the government. There is good reason to identify Bay as the Irsu of the text. That a foreigner could acquire so important a voice in Egyptian government attests to the sorry state of affairs during these "empty years" that saw the collapse of the Nineteenth Dynasty.

2.

The throne of Egypt stood vacant for several months after the death of Tawosret (x-rays of her mummy showed no features of special interest). Contenders for control must have engaged in considerable back-room politics before a certain Setnakht mustered enough support in 1200 B.C. to have himself crowned king. Nothing is known of his origins or his two-year reign. He was an elderly man, and, from the first, his son, Ramesses III, took a major part in the affairs of state. Ramesses III was later to describe his father as the ruler who saved Egypt's crumbling government, but in fact it was Ramesses III himself who was able to restore a small part of his country's former greatness.

Ramesses III was very much like Ramesses II in character, and he was continually trying to emulate the latter's tedious braggadocio in long and exaggerated texts. Fortunately for Egypt, his boasts were not quite so hollow, for he was a much better military commander. During the first eleven years of his reign he concentrated on strengthening Egypt's borders and fought several major battles against enemies who, driven by hunger during years of famine in their homeland, sought control of the lush Nile Valley. After these battles had been fought and won, he confidently abandoned military activity and devoted himself to Egypt's internal affairs. He said of himself:

> I planted the entire land with trees and greenery and I let the people sit in their shade; I caused the woman of Egypt to travel freely wherever she wanted, and no foreigner or anyone of the road molested her. I allowed the infantry and the chariotry to settle down during my time. . . .[5]

Yet papyri of the period have preserved for us tales of woefully corrupt administrators, of strikes called by workmen in the necropolis, even of a conspiracy to murder the king himself.

The years of Ramesses III saw an already failing Egyptian government lose even more of its authority and wealth owing to a major new development in the ancient

Near East: the coming of iron. In a very few years this new metal replaced gold as a standard of trade, and Egypt, having no ore of its own, found its economy unstable and badly inflationary. It was during this period that tomb robbing became a major activity at Thebes. The continued abundance of Egypt's crops could not offset the dire effects of rising prices and increasingly inefficient administration.

The men who worked as laborers and craftsmen on government projects were hurt particularly badly by this inflation. A sizable number, who were employed by the throne to dig, carve, decorate, and maintain the tombs in the necropolis of western Thebes, decided, after several years of what they believed to be disregard by the government, to make a number of demands—for more water carriers, bakers, fishermen, and the like—to provide for their needs. These demands were granted, but for reasons of inefficiency or shortage, the workmen's daily salary, paid in grain, suddenly stopped. For sixty days the men received nothing from the government, and in mid-November, 1170 B.C., they went on strike. They left the necropolis in a group and refused to return. A promise of immediate action, passed down from the pharaoh himself, had no effect; they countered by establishing a picket line inside the Ramesseum, an important temple nearby. "We have reached this place because of hunger," they chanted, "because of thirst, without clothing, without oil, without flesh, without vegetables. Write to the Pharaoh, our good lord, about it and write to the Vizier, our superior. Act so that we may live!"[6] Their action won them half of their back salary. But a few days later grain deliveries again were halted, and another series of strikes and protest rallies were held. Government officials alternately sympathized and chastised them. Invariably they promised help that was not forthcoming.

The workmen went to the High Priest of Amon across the river and pleaded for food from the temple's stores. The High Priest argued that their grain must come from their leaders, not from him. At last the vizier agreed to pay them a part of their salary, presumably from his own stores, and it is assumed (for the records are incomplete) that the men returned to work. But the action the workmen took and the slow, inept responses of the bureaucracy clearly indicate that while the discontent may have been calmed temporarily, its causes were still present and would continue to generate problems for the country.

In the last years of his reign Ramesses III faced a problem far greater than the strikes. One of his secondary wives, a woman named Tiy, together with several officials of the court and members of the harim to which she belonged (the king had several), plotted to assassinate him in order that her son, Pentwere, be made ruler instead of the rightful heir, Ramesses IV. One of her cohorts in this scheme was asked by the harim to "stir up the people, foment hostility, come to make a revolution against your lord."[7]

The conspirators used a number of devices, including magic, to avoid detection, but in vain. Their plot was discovered and they were ordered to stand trial. This was shortly before the king's death after a reign of thirty-two years. All evidence shows that his death was a natural one.

Although the architecture and art of Ramesses III show a marked decline in quality, his enormous tomb, carved in the Valley of the Kings, contains numerous scenes of great interest. Some of them are scenes of daily life, which usually are found only with non-royal burials. His mummy is that of an old man, about sixty-five, and it is still well wrapped—the work of later restorers.

X-rays reveal statuettes of three of the Four Sons of Horus in the left side of the thoracic cage. Taken both from the front and the side, the x-rays pinpoint the location of these objects, but it is unlikely they will ever be removed. There is too much chance the body might be damaged in such an operation. In all probability these figures, made of wax, are either uninscribed or briefly inscribed with religious texts already known from other sources. Their purpose was purely religious and therefore traditional.

Dentally, Ramesses III bears strong similarity to Seti II and to later rulers of this period, with the same slight degree of prognathism. The third molars (the wisdom teeth) are not erupted, but this is by no means an uncommon occurrence in peoples of any period, as a good many Westerners of the twentieth century can attest.

The arms of the king are folded over the chest in typical fashion, but the hands are open. At the time of Seti I, whose mummy shows this same characteristic, this was an unusual occurrence. After the reign of Ramesses III it was common.

The remaining eighty-one years of the Twentieth Dynasty were ruled over by eight kings, most of whom reigned very briefly. These were years that saw the authority of the throne decline steadily until its powers were divided between the pharaoh and the priests of Amon, with the priests actually controlling most of the country's wealth.

Ramesses III was succeeded by his son Ramesses IV, who ruled only six years. During that time he added his name to many existing monuments and recorded that

8368 workmen were necessary to quarry stone for his own buildings. Such a statement suggests an affluent and settled time, but other texts, which describe thefts and malfeasance in office, bribery, and trials of adulterers, belie this. It was, in short, a time no better than the decades that immediately preceded it.

The tomb of Ramesses IV, carved in the Valley of the Kings, is neither the largest nor the most impressive there, but it has particular interest: a plan of it, giving exact dimensions and drawn approximately to scale, has been preserved on a fragment of papyrus. A series of notes were written on it by the supervising scribe, explaining the functions of each chamber. The largest room is described in this way:

> [Its] door is fastened.
>
> The House of Gold, wherein One rests, of 16 cubits; breadth, of 16 cubits; height, of 10 cubits; being drawn with outlines, graven with the chisel, filled with colors, and completed; and being provided with the equipment of His Majesty (he lives, prosperous, is in health!) on every side of it, together with the Divine Ennead which is in the Dē't.
>
> Total, beginning from the First Corridor to the House of Gold, 136 cubits, 2 palms. . . .[8]

While a study of these dimensions has shown that they are not exact, the plan and specifications are surprisingly accurate. It is one of a very few such documents known from ancient Egypt.

The mummy of Ramesses IV, rather sloppily rewrapped by later priests, shows a large abdominal incision sewn together with a twisted piece of bandage. As with Siptah, the embalmers of Ramesses packed the abdominal cavity with dried lichens, the only other time this alternative to the more usual method is known to have occurred.

Ramesses IV shows only slight resemblance to the earlier kings of the dynasty. His teeth are in unusually good condition, and the incisors protrude to a greater degree than those of his predecessors. Only his nose suggests any relationship to them: although flattened by the embalmers, it is quite as prominent as those of earlier kings. Ramesses IV and Ramesses V were similar in general appearance.

Ramesses V, who succeeded his father in 1160 B.C., probably reigned only four years. The only sources available for the study of his reign are a mummy and a papyrus.

The mummy of Ramesses V, discovered in the tomb of Amenhotep II, shows papular eruptions on the skin, which suggest that the king suffered—and probably died—from smallpox. The diagnosis, admittedly based on the distribution and form of these eruptions rather than on laboratory examination (still impossible to conduct), seemed convincing to Smith, and the Michigan Expedition cannot offer an alternative diagnosis. The unusually large size of the scrotum suggests that the king also suffered from an inguinal hernia.

Like those of Siptah and Ramesses IV, the mummy of Ramesses V represents a departure from the normal practice of filling the abdomen with resin-soaked bandages. But unlike the two earlier rulers, whose bodies were packed with lichens, Ramesses V was simply stuffed with sawdust that had portions of internal organs embedded in it. This new technique quickly gained favor in Egypt, and later kings would also have the complete viscera replaced in the abdomen after embalming, with sawdust used for packing. There was an aromatic scent to the body, probably due to some of the spices used in this packing process, clearly noticeable when the museum case was opened.

Dentally, there is little doubt that the king died in his early thirties. The teeth show very little wear, and the third molars, which must have erupted only a few years before death, are in particularly good condition.

The left femur shows a pronounced post-mortem fracture, doubtless caused by later grave robbers, who also hacked their way through the bandages and even the flesh in their search for objects.

A papyrus recording events in the early years of an unnamed king is likely to belong to the reign of either Ramesses V or VI, most probably Ramesses VI. It is a journal kept by the scribe overseeing work on the king's tomb and tells of what can only be an episode of civil war in Egypt. "The people who are enemies came and reached Per-nebyt," it reads. "They destroyed everything which was there and buried its people, so it is rumored." The scribe was ordered to place guards at the king's tomb in case the insurrection came closer to Thebes, and a few days later the chief of police told the foreman, "Do not go up [to the Valley of the Kings] until you see what has happened."[9]

It is very possible that the accession of Ramesses VI to the throne may have been one reason for such an insurrection, for he was not the son of Ramesses V but rather his uncle, a son of Ramesses III. One cannot help wondering if a struggle for power within the Ramesside line had occurred and the rightful heir had lost.

Many of the mummies examined in the Cairo museum had been badly damaged by tomb robbers, but none worse than the mummy of Ramesses VI. According to

Smith, "The head and trunk were literally hacked to pieces and when the mummy came to be rewrapped it was necessary to obtain a board—a rough piece of coffin—on which to tie the fragments of the body and give them some semblance of the form of a mummy."[10] When Smith first unwrapped the mummy, in fact, he found bits and pieces of other bodies, including the right hand of a woman, thrown into the pile of torn linen that had been used in restoring the proper form. A severed arm was rewrapped on the thigh, and one of the hip bones lay on the neck. An ax had broken through the elbow, the neck had been severed from the body, the face smashed, and knife cuts covered the head. Like many other kings of the New Kingdom, he had pierced ears and was partially bald.

It is tempting to surmise that Ramesses VI was not the rightful heir to the throne and after his death (from unknown causes) his body was attacked by his enemies. But as yet there is no definite evidence to suggest that anyone other than later tomb robbers was responsible.

The condition of the mummy made it almost impossible to obtain information from x-rays. They do show, however, that the king died sometime in early middle age, for his teeth are only moderately worn. And as might be expected of such a distant relation, he bears only slight similarity to Ramesses IV and V.

Of the remaining kings of the Twentieth Dynasty, little more is known than their names. Even the order of the kings is in some doubt. It seems likely, for example, that Ramesses VII ruled after Ramesses VIII. The dynasty ended with the last of the Ramesside kings, Ramesses XI, in 1085 B.C.

❦ 3.

The Twenty-first Dynasty is generally believed to have begun around 1085–1070 B.C. and to have ended about 945–939 B.C., but few Egyptologists are in agreement about its internal chronology and genealogy, and the scanty records of the period have been subject to a number of interpretations. The detailed study of the familial and chronological interrelations of the High Priests and kings of the period made in the 1960s by the American Egyptologist Edward Wente of the Oriental Institute at the University of Chicago offers the most convincing reconstruction to date, though it too is perhaps subject to change in detail.[11]

Throughout most of Egyptian history, the priests and the temples they served had received a share of the agricultural produce and tribute of their country. During the years preceding the Twenty-first Dynasty, this share had increased to such an extent that temple estates controlled over 25 per cent of all Egypt's resources, and the income from these resources was almost completely tax exempt. By far the largest portion of this wealth—nearly 75 per cent—went to the Temple of Amon at Thebes; and, building upon this solid economic foundation, the priests of Amon were able to reach out and gain control of more and more of Egypt's civil administration and of powers formerly held by the throne.

During the reign of Ramesses XI, last king of the Twentieth Dynasty, the High Priest of Amon had become so powerful that he proved a real threat to the throne, and a serious attempt was made to have him removed from office. When this occurred the authority of the High Priest was not returned to the king but was assumed by a certain Pinehas, one of the leaders of the movement. Pinehas apparently suffered delusions of grandeur. He might have succeeded in gaining control of all Egypt; but for reasons that can only be guessed, he quickly fell into disfavor and disappeared. One of those involved in the plot against him was the new High Priest of Amon, Herihor.

Herihor, possibly the son of a former High Priest, began solidifying his position by strengthening the social and political powers of the Temple of Amon. The throne, after years of decline, was in no position to argue. The priesthood continued to chip away at royal powers, and the Oracles of Amon, divine instructions interpreted by the High Priest, wielded more authority than the pharaoh. In addition, the king had moved the Royal Residence from the traditional centers of Memphis and Thebes to Tanis, a city in the eastern delta quite removed from the mainstream of Egyptian social and political activity, and this move in itself effectively limited the throne's power to Lower Egypt.

Herihor, to all intents and purposes, had gained control of the most powerful position in Egypt. Even though the king continued to sit upon the throne, Herihor was certain enough of his power to include on temple walls scenes showing himself the equal of the king. He even wrote his name in the royal cartouche (an oval, symbolizing a loop of rope with tied ends, in which the king's name was written) preceded by titles formerly reserved for the Pharaoh alone. With his rise to power, the priests of Amon became the effective rulers of Egypt.

Although Herihor assumed the titles of royalty, he did not actually depose Ramesses XI. Probably there was no need for such action since the weakness of the throne and its remote geographic location made it unlikely that it could pose any serious threat to the power of the temple. However, to further strengthen his claim, Heri-hor married his sister Nodjme. In doing so, he made certain that the position of High Priest of Amon would be filled by hereditary right, not by royal appointment. They had two sons, Smendes and Piankh.

Little is known of Nodjme, but hers is the earliest mummy from this period, and it shows a number of major changes in the embalming techniques.

Smith has suggested that it was the discovery in Ramesside times of the bodies of earlier kings that brought about the changes. Again, as in the early dynastic period, the sudden realization that accepted techniques were not working prompted new and more elaborate attempts. The packing of the mummy was now done in such a way that an almost portrait-like quality was achieved, with artificial eyes inserted into the empty sockets and red ochre applied to the skin to restore a lifelike color. Even defects of form such as sunken cheeks or emaciated limbs were corrected.

The mummy of Nodjme, one of the first to benefit from these new techniques, had packing inserted only in the facial cavity, but in such quantity that the face seems round and almost puffy. Artificial eyes of white and black stone were inserted, and new eyebrows of real hair were carefully glued in place. The artificial eyes show clearly in the x-rays, as do four wax figures of the Four Sons of Horus and a large scarab inserted into the thoracic cage.

Nodjme's dentition is not particularly good, but there is little unusual about it except an unerupted wisdom tooth in the right maxilla and a displaced wisdom tooth in the mandible. Bad dentition is a rather minor point, however, when one sees this almost doll-like figure. She is so well preserved, so carefully wrapped, so beautifully decorated, that she seems only to be sleeping.

Smendes became king upon the death of Ramesses XI.

The son of Herihor and Nodjme, he was married to a certain Tentamun and perhaps because of her parentage assumed a throne to which he had no hereditary right. It is probably this same Tentamun who was the mother of Henttowy; the latter is referred to as the "King's bodily Daughter, Great King's Wife, King's Mother, Mother of the God's Wife of Amon, Mother of the God's Votaress of Amon, God's Mother of Khonsu the Child, and First Great Chief of the Concubines of Amon."[12] Much of the knowledge of this period is based upon what is known of Henttowy, and it may be fairly said that she is one of the most important figures. Henttowy lived for some time and was married to her cousin Pinudjem I, who succeeded his father Piankh as High Priest of Amon.

During this period, as we have seen, the Temple of Amon wielded great power and justified its actions by claiming them to be based directly upon the Oracles of Amon-Re. Questions were submitted by the priests to the god's statue at Thebes, and the resulting oracle was considered the final answer in all matters. There is a record, dating from the priesthood of Piankh, describing how an appointment to a high temple post was decided by this method: when the great god Amon-Re, carried on his processional bark, was stopped before the candidate he nodded his approval. Only the priest, of course, could make a statue, even the statue of a god, nod.

Although Pinudjem I was certainly the most powerful individual in Egypt, there is little doubt that his wife, as chief concubine of the god, also held great authority. Henttowy's status was further enhanced since she provided a bond of kinship between the throne and the priesthood and because hereditary rights were probably reckoned matrilineally at this time.

The techniques used in the mummification of Henttowy were almost exactly the same as those used for Nodjme but the results were inferior. Here the cheeks were so overpacked with a mixture of fat and soda that the face has burst open. Today she presents a grisly picture.

A large piece of gold was affixed to the abdominal incision, and one small statue of a Son of Horus lay inside the thorax. Aromatic sawdust was used to pack the abdomen (it still offers a most pleasant aroma), very fine linen was used in the wrapping, and some care was taken to restore the thighs to a lifelike fullness. Her large and elaborate coiffure was made of tightly twisted strands of black string.

The marriage of Henttowy and Pinudjem I (who had at least one other wife) produced four offspring. Psusennes I, perhaps their youngest son, married his sister Mutnutme, and from this marriage came the later kings of the dynasty. Their brother Menkheperre assumed the title of High Priest of Amon and married a woman called Esemkhebe.

Esemkhebe's mummy had been so beautifully wrapped by the embalmers that Smith decided not to open it. Again, x-rays provided the first glimpses beneath the wrappings. A small amulet lay on her neck, one of less distinct form on the right arm, and on the forehead was another small object. The teeth were worn, and the molars showed what might well have been caries, if the lesions were not the result of post-mortem damage. The third molar had been displaced by some injury. The knees showed evidence of degenerative arthritis.

Makare, whom some believe to have been Esemkhebe's half-sister, apparently assumed an even more important role in the religious hierarchy than earlier women of the dynasty, for in a relief in the Khonsu temple she is shown wearing a far more elaborate head-dress than Henttowy and is given the title of God's Wife of Amon at Karnak, the highest position a woman in the temple could attain.

Makare died at a relatively early age, and an examination of her mummy indicates that she died either during childbirth or very shortly thereafter. Even the packing of her abdomen by the embalmers was done to indicate that fact. It had been assumed that Makare's child was a girl named Moutemhet who died in infancy and was buried with her mother. It is now clear that the name Moutemhet belonged to Makare herself and that the small mummy placed in her sarcophagus is not a child at all but a female hamadryas baboon. Presumably, therefore, Makare's child survived its mother, but scholars are completely ignorant both of its career and of its father. They are not even certain that Makare was married—the God's Wife of Amon, some believe, was supposed to be a virgin—and it is quite possible that the child was a result of the ritual temple prostitution later writers describe as having been prevalent at this time.

A number of possible explanations for the burial of a baboon with Makare come to mind, but none seems completely convincing. The baboon was associated in Egyptian religion with Thoth, the god of learning and knowledge and science. In later times a small piece of cloth with a baboon painted on it was often included in burials (a so-called hypocephalus) to provide "inner warmth" to the otherwise cold corpse. But from such associations of baboons to the actual burial of one with the mummy is a fairly big step.

Some scholars have wondered if perhaps the baboon was in fact a substitute for Makare's infant. If she had died during childbirth, they argue, might it not have seemed appropriate to bury at least a substitute child with her for the afterlife? There is no evidence for this, but it is an interesting—and not unpleasant—idea.

Of the later rulers of the Twenty-first Dynasty almost nothing is known. With the death of this dynasty's last ruler, Egypt fell into the hands of a foreign group called the Meshwesh, who probably came from Libya. Not even the priesthood had sufficient power to withstand the takeover.

Dynastic Egypt lasted nine more dynasties. Mummification continued to be practiced, but it was largely an inaccurate imitation of the techniques of the New Kingdom.

It was really the collapse of New Kingdom Egypt rather than the fall of the Thirtieth Dynasty some five hundred years later that saw the vibrant and independent culture of Egypt come to an end. From then on, Egypt's culture was to be more borrowed than indigenous.

CONCLUSION

The results of the Michigan Expedition's project are of considerable importance both for Egyptology and medical history. The x-rays of the mummies have shed light on the various diseases from which Egypt's rulers suffered and have provided a much better picture of ancient medical and dental problems than texts alone could give. They have shown that the previous calculations of the ages at which various pharaohs died are incorrect, and therefore parts of the chronology of ancient Egypt will have to be altered, in some cases drastically. The x-rays have also shown that the genetic relationships among the members of the ruling families are by no means as clear-cut as once was thought. While the kings of the early Eighteenth Dynasty closely resemble one another, as do those of the early Nineteenth Dynasty, an enormous difference between the two groups is evident. Clearly the rulers of ancient Egypt do not form a single genetic line, and the royal family tree will have to be revised.

Through x-rays, even information on cultural practices were revealed. It was found that circumcision,
thought to be universal, did not always occur. Statuettes
and other religious symbols and jewelry were discovered
inside of bodies.

As the project continues, it is hoped that even more
information will be revealed about how the ancient
Egyptian ruling class lived and died. Such studies have
value for modern man. Through a better understanding
of the way of life of ancient Egypt, the way in which its
people sought to deal with disease and the eternal question of death—in short, through a better understanding
of his ancestors—man shall be able to understand better
the nature of his own problems, to find their solution,
and ultimately better to understand himself.

REFERENCE NOTES

CHRONOLOGY

KINSHIP CHARTS

INDEX

Reference Notes

ONE: THE MUMMY

1. G. Elliot Smith, "The Royal Mummies," *Catalogue Général des Antiquités du Egyptiennes du Musée du Caire, Nos. 61051–61100* (Cairo: Service des Antiquités de l'Egypte, 1912), pp. iii–iv.

2. Geoffrey F. Walker and Charles J. Kowalski, "A Two-Dimensional Coordinate Model for the Quantification, Description, Analysis, Prediction and Simulation of Craniofacial Growth," *Growth*, 35 (1971), 191–211; James E. Harris, Paul V. Ponitz, M. Samir Loutfy, "Orthodontics' Contribution to UNESCO's Campaign to Save the Monuments of Nubia: A 1970 Field Report," *American Journal of Orthodontics*, 58 (December, 1970), 578–96.

TWO: THE MAKING OF THE MUMMY

1. Quoted in R. Engelbach and Douglas Derry, "Mummification," *Annales du Service des Antiquités de l'Egypte*, 41 (1942), 236–38.

2. Quoted in G[rafton] Elliot Smith and Warren R. Dawson, *Egyptian Mummies* (New York: Dial Press, 1923), p. 62.

181

3. Zaki Iskander, personal communication, 1971.

4. Dr. Iskander will publish a detailed analysis of these techniques in the forthcoming technical report of the University of Michigan Expedition.

5. Quoted in Smith and Dawson, *op. cit.*, p. 66.

6. Quoted in E. A. T. W. Budge, *The Mummy: A Handbook of Egyptian Funerary Archaeology* (Cambridge: Cambridge University Press, 1925), p. 290.

7. Serge Sauneron, *Rituel de l'Embaumement, Pap. Boulaq 3 and Pap. Louvre 5. 158* (Cairo: Service des Antiquités de l'Egypte, 1952), p. 18.

8. Quoted in Thomas J. Pettigrew, *A History of Egyptian Mummies, and an Account of the Worship and Embalming of Sacred Animals by the Egyptians . . .* (London: Longman, Rees, Orme, Brown, Green and Longman, 1834), p. 11.

THREE: THE MUMMY DEFILED

1. Giovanni Belzoni, *Narrative of the Operations and Recent Discoveries within the Pyramids, Temples, Tombs and Excavations in Egypt and Nubia . . .* (London: John Murray, 1820), pp. 158, 181.

2. J. Robichon and A. Varille, *Le Temple du Scribe royal Amenhotep fils de Hapou* (Cairo: Institut Français d'Archéologie Orientale, 1936), pp. 4–7.

3. Gaston Maspero, *La Trouvaille de Deir el-Bahari.* (Cairo: Imprimerie Nouvelle du "Moniteur Egyptien," 1883), p. 9. See also his *Les Momies Royales de Deir el-Bahari* (Cairo: *Mémoires . . . Mission Archéologique Française au Caire*, I, 2, 1887), pp. 511–788.

4. James Henry Breasted, *Ancient Records of Egypt, Historical Documents* (five vols., *Ancient Records,* 2nd series; Chicago: University of Chicago Press, 1906), II, 106.

5. For hieroglyphic texts, see T. Eric Peet, *The Great Tomb-Robberies of the Twentieth Egyptian Dynasty* (Oxford: Oxford University Press, 1930); translations are by Kent R. Weeks.

6. *Ibid.*

7. *Ibid.*

8. *Ibid.*

9. *Ibid.*

10. *Ibid.*

11. Breasted, *op. cit.,* IV, 665.

12. Howard Carter, "Report on the Robbery of the Tomb of Amenothes II, Biban el Moluk," *Annales du Service des Antiquités Egyptiennes,* III (1902), 115–20.

13. *Ibid.*

14. Miriam Lichtheim, "The Song of the Harpers," *Journal of Near Eastern Studies,* XXIV (1945), 192–93.

FOUR: THE PHARAOH'S MUMMY

1. Smith, "The Royal Mummies," *Catalogue Général des Antiquités* . . ., pp. 2–3.

2. Herbert Winlock, "The Tombs of the Kings of the Seventeenth Dynasty at Thebes," *Journal of Egyptian Archaeology,* X (1924), 248–249.

3. Breasted, *Ancient Records of Egypt* . . . , II, p. 41, 108.

4. *Ibid.,* p. 142, 341.

5. Donald B. Redford, *A History and Chronology of the Eighteenth Dynasty of Egypt: Seven Studies* (Toronto: University of Toronto Press, 1967), pp. 66 ff.

6. William C. Hayes, *The Scepter of Egypt: A Background for the Study of the Egyptian Antiquities in the Metropolitan Museum of Art* (Two vols.; Cambridge, Mass.: Harvard University Press, 1953), II, 116.

7. *Ibid.,* p. 140.

8. James Pritchard, ed., *Ancient Near Eastern Texts Relating to the Old Testament* (Princeton: Princeton University Press, 1950), p. 449.

9. Cyril Aldred, *The Pharoah of Egypt Akhenaton: A New Study* (London: Thames and Hudson, 1968), p. 137. See also Cyril Aldred and A. T. Sandison, "The Pharaoh Akhenaton, A Problem in Egyptology and Pathology," *Bulletin of the History of Medicine,* XXXVI (1962), 293–316.

10. Aldred and Sandison, *op. cit.,* pp. 314–15.

11. R.G. Harrison, "An Anatomical Examination of the Pharaonic Remains Purported to be Akhenaton," *Journal of Egyptian Archaeology*, LII (1966), 95–119.

12. *Ibid.*,

13. R.G. Harrison, R.C. Connolly, A. Abdalla, "Kinship of Smenkhare and Tutankhamon Demonstrated Serologically," *Nature*, 224 (1969), 325–26.

FIVE: THE MORTAL MUMMY

1. John A. Wilson, *The Culture of Ancient Egypt* (Chicago: University of Chicago Press, Phoenix Books, 1951), p. 243.

2. Hayes, *The Scepter of Egypt . . .* , II, 334.

3. Smith, "The Royal Mummies," *Catalogue Général des Antiquités . . .* , p. 63.

4. Breasted, *Ancient Records of Egypt . . .* , IV, 398; Alan Gardiner, *Egypt of the Pharaohs* (Oxford: Oxford University Press, 1961), p. 281.

5. Breasted, *op. cit.*, IV, 410.

6. Wilson, *op. cit.*, p. 276.

7. Breasted, *op. cit.*, IV, 427.

8. Howard Carter and Alan H. Gardiner, "The Tomb of Ramesses IV and the Turin Plan of a Royal Tomb," *Journal of Egyptian Archaeology*, IV (1917), 139.

9. J. Černy, "Egypt from the Death of Ramesses II to the End of the Twenty-first Dynasty," *Cambridge Ancient History* (2nd ed.; Cambridge: Cambridge University Press, 1965), II, 10. (Chapter 35, issued as a separate fascicule.)

10. Smith, *op. cit.*, p. 92.

11. Edward F. Wente, "On the Chronology of the Twenty-first Dynasty," *Journal of Near Eastern Studies*, XXVI (1967), 155–76.

12. *Ibid.*, pp. 157–59.

A Chronology
of Ancient Egypt

(Names of rulers are given only for the
periods represented in the collection of royal
mummies in the Egyptian Museum. Names of women
are printed in *italic* type.)

	DATES B.C.
UNIFICATION OF EGYPT	ca. 3100
EARLY DYNASTIC PERIOD (Dynasties I and II)	3100–2686
OLD KINGDOM (Dynasties III through VI)	2686–2181
FIRST INTERMEDIATE PERIOD (Dynasties VII through X)	2181–2050
MIDDLE KINGDOM (Dynasties XI and XII)	2050–1786
SECOND INTERMEDIATE PERIOD (Dynasties XIII through Early XVII)	1786–1567
NEW KINGDOM (Late Dynasty XVII through Dynasty XX)	1600–1085

Khayan
Senakhtenre Tao; *Tetisheri*
Seqenenre Tao; *Ahhotep I*
Kamose

NEW KINGDOM (continued)

Eighteenth Dynasty

Ahmose I	1570–1546
Ahmenhotep I	1546–1526
Thutmosis I	1526–1512
Thutmosis II	1512–1504
Hatshepsut	1503–1482
Thutmosis III	1504–1450
Amenhotep II	1450–1425
Thutmosis IV	1425–1417
Amenhotep III	1417–1379
Amenhotep IV (Akhenaton)	1379–1362
Smenkhare	1364–1361
Tutankhaton (Tutankhamon)	1361–1352
Ay	1352–1348
Horemhab	1348–1320

Nineteenth Dynasty   1320–1200

Ramesses I	1320–1318
Seti I	1318–1304
Ramesses II	1304–1237
Merenptah	1236–1223
Amenmesses	1222–1217
Seti II	1216–1210
Siptah	1209–1200

Twentieth Dynasty   1200–1085

Setnakht	1200–1198
Ramesses III	1198–1166
Ramesses IV	1166–1160
Ramesses V	1160–1156
Ramesses VI	1156–1148
Ramesses VII	1148–1147
Ramesses VIII	1147–1140
Ramesses IX	1140–1121
Ramesses X	1121–1113
Ramesses XI	1113–1085

POST-EMPIRE PERIOD

Twenty-first Dynasty   1085–945

At Tanis

Smendes
Psusennes I
Amenemope
Siamun
Psusennes II

At Thebes (Priest-Kings)

Herihor
Pinankh
Pinudjem I
Masahert
Menkheperre
Pinudjem II

Kinship Charts

The charts which follow indicate the relationships of the principal rulers discussed in the text; they are not complete family trees. Names of rulers are printed in **boldface;** names of women in *italics.* Where "m." occurs between two names it indicates marriage. In a few instances names of individuals have been repeated within the charts for clarity; these are marked with asterisks (*).

LATE-SEVENTEENTH-DYNASTY AND EIGHTEENTH-DYNASTY RULERS

Family of Ahmose I

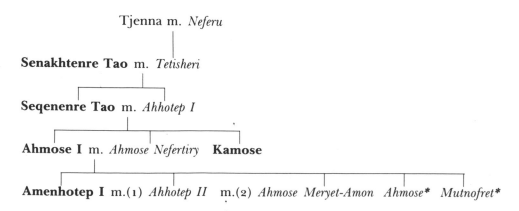

Family of Thutmosis I

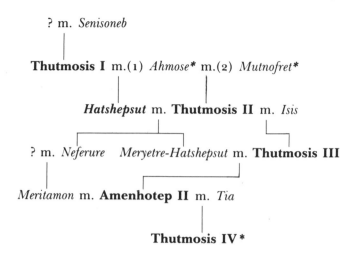

```
                    ? m. Senisoneb
                           │
     Thutmosis I m.(1) Ahmose* m.(2) Mutnofret*
                    │                 │
          Hatshepsut m. Thutmosis II m. Isis
                ┌─────────┤          └─┐
     ? m. Neferure   Meryetre-Hatshepsut m. Thutmosis III
          │      ┌──────────────────────┘
 Meritamon m. Amenhotep II m. Tia
                      │
              Thutmosis IV*
```

Family of Thutmosis IV

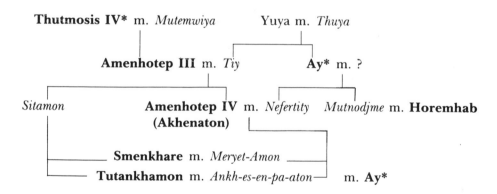

```
  Thutmosis IV* m. Mutemwiya          Yuya m. Thuya
                │                  ┌────────┴──────┐
        Amenhotep III m. Tiy              Ay* m. ?
   ┌─────────────────┤              ┌───────┴────┐
 Sitamon     Amenhotep IV m. Nefertity   Mutnodjme m. Horemhab
             (Akhenaton)    │
         ┌─── Smenkhare m. Meryet-Amon ───┐
         └─── Tutankhamon m. Ankh-es-en-pa-aton ──┘  m. Ay*
```

NINETEENTH-DYNASTY RULERS

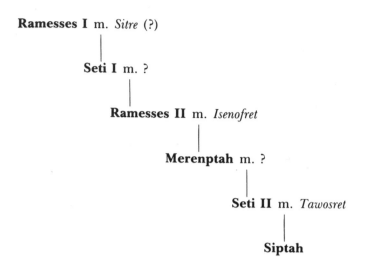

Ramesses I m. *Sitre* (?)

    Seti I m. ?

        Ramesses II m. *Isenofret*

            Merenptah m. ?

                Seti II m. *Tawosret*

                    Siptah

TWENTIETH-DYNASTY RULERS

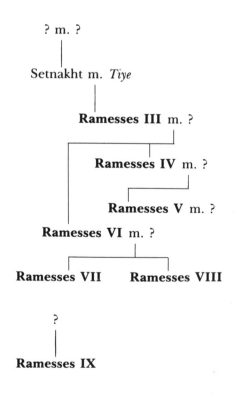

? m. ?

  Setnakht m. *Tiye*

    Ramesses III m. ?

      Ramesses IV m. ?

        Ramesses V m. ?

  Ramesses VI m. ?

Ramesses VII   **Ramesses VIII**

?

Ramesses IX

TENTATIVE RECONSTRUCTION OF THE HIGH PRIESTS OF AMON DURING THE TWENTY-FIRST DYNASTY

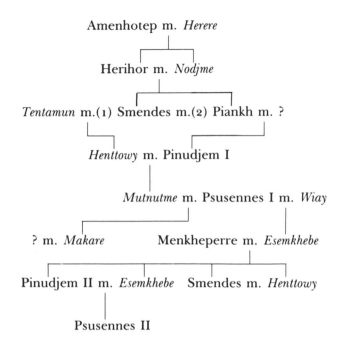

Amenhotep m. *Herere*

Herihor m. *Nodjme*

Tentamun m.(1) Smendes m.(2) Piankh m. ?

Henttowy m. Pinudjem I

Mutnutme m. Psusennes I m. *Wiay*

? m. *Makare*   Menkheperre m. *Esemkhebe*

Pinudjem II m. *Esemkhebe*   Smendes m. *Henttowy*

Psusennes II

Index